1 & 2
THESSALONIANS

P Harding

JOHN RITCHIE LTD
CHRISTIAN PUBLICATIONS

40 Beansburn, Kilmarnock, Scotland

ISBN-13: 978 1 904064 93 0
ISBN-10: 1 904064 93 0

Copyright © 2010 by John Ritchie Ltd.
40 Beansburn, Kilmarnock, Scotland

Typeset by John Ritchie Ltd., Kilmarnock
Printed by Bell & Bain Ltd., Glasgow

Contents

I would like to express my appreciation to my three daughters, Christine Raggett of Palapye, Botswana; Elaine Raggett of Wilmslow, Chester, England; and Andrea Williams of Newton Stewart, Scotland for the original checking of the articles.

The original articles which formed this book originally appeared in 'Assembly Testimony'.

1 Thessalonians

The city of Thessalonica was situated on the famous Egnatian way and was a key city in Macedonia, being its chief port. It was therefore strategically and commercially important. Its population was mostly Gentile but a large company of Jews with their Synagogue exerted a strong proselytising influence upon the Gentiles. The gospel came to Thessalonica through the apostle Paul and his companions and some of the Jews and many of the Gentiles were saved and an assembly planted (Acts 17:1-4). The length of their stay in Thessalonica is not stated but as a result of the opposition which arose, Paul and Silas were compelled to leave (Acts 17:5-10). Paul, greatly concerned about the newly planted assembly, sent Timothy from Athens back to Thessalonica to encourage the saints and to see how the assembly was progressing (1 Thessalonians 3:1-2). The report, which he received at Corinth (Acts 18:5), was encouraging and thus, through the prompting of the gracious Spirit of God, he writes this first epistle to the assembly. We can divide the epistle into three sections:- Chapters 1-3 Historical, Chapter 4 Doctrinal and Chapter 5 Instructional. In the Historical section we have how the gospel was received (chapter 1), how the servants conducted themselves (chapter 2), and where the servants went and how they acted (chapter 3).

CHAPTER 1

How the Gospel was Received

After the opening salutation (Verse 1) the apostle Paul expresses gratitude to God (Verses 2-4) and rehearses the result of the gospel coming to the Thessalonians (Verses 5-10). We can divide the chapter into three sections:- Verses 1-4 The Expression of Gratitude, Verses 5-7 The Entrance of the Gospel into Thessalonica and Verses 8-10 The Expansion of the Gospel.

Verses 1-4 The Expression of Gratitude
Verse 1. **"Paul, and Silvanus, and Timothy,"** Although Paul is undoubtedly the writer of this epistle he links himself with his fellow-labourers. How delightful to see three servants from different age groups, different backgrounds and different abilities being linked harmoniously together in service for God - no jealousy, no competition, no bitterness. There was a common interest and a common purpose. How important harmony is to the work of God. There is no mention of Paul's apostleship here since this was not in question in Thessalonica. Silvanus (Silas) was a prophet (Acts 15:32) and, like Paul, was a Jew and a Roman citizen (Acts 16:37-38). He joined Paul for the second missionary journey (Acts 15:40) and was among the first to bring the gospel to Europe. Timotheus (Timothy) had a Jewish mother but a Gentile father (Acts 16:1). He was a young man from Lystra (Acts 16:1; 1 Timothy 4:12), saved through the preaching of Paul and well reported of by the brethren in Lystra and Iconium (Acts 16:2). Timothy is mentioned in all Paul's epistles except Galatians, Ephesians and Titus. Silvanus is only mentioned here and in 2 Thessalonians and 2 Corinthians.

"unto the church of the Thessalonians" When Paul and his companions arrived at Thessalonica there was a Jewish Synagogue and a Heathen Temple there but through the preaching of the gospel a Christian Assembly was planted. The word "church" is better translated 'assembly' and means a company called out - called out for a purpose. The words "church of" are peculiar to 1 & 2 Thessalonians (except the Colossians 4:16) and bring before us the principle of believers in a locality, gathered unto the Name of the Lord Jesus. A called out company bearing a collective testimony to all the truth of God in that locality for the pleasure and glory of God.

"in God the Father and in the Lord Jesus Christ:" This denotes the atmosphere of divine Persons, the deity of Christ being implied in the expression. The assembly was grounded and existed in the sphere and power of God the Father and of the Lord Jesus Christ. The first expression is a contrast to the heathen temple (paganism) and the second expression is a contrast to the Jewish temple (Judaism). In God the Father - indicates relationship and shows that the newly planted assembly was in the tender care of the Father. This would be an encouragement to them since they were passing through a time of persecution (see 2:14; 3:4). In the Lord Jesus Christ - indicates redemption and shows the source of power for testimony. It may also show that the assembly acknowledged and confessed Jesus Christ as Lord.

"Grace be unto you, and peace," The desire of Paul for them. Grace, the transforming power of God, operating in the lives of those who are unworthy. It was this grace which was necessary for the Thessalonians to continue in the pathway of the will of God in the face of opposition and persecution. It is this grace which is vital in order for every child of God to live for Him in every circumstance of life. Peace (inward tranquillity) despite outward circumstances - a state of well being in spite of the persecution.

"from God our Father, and the Lord Jesus Christ." The source of all that is necessary to enable the child of God to live for the pleasure and glory of God.

Verse 2. **"We give thanks to God always for you all,"** The expression of thanksgiving for what the grace and power of God had wrought in Thessalonica - gratitude to God for what He had produced in the lives of these Thessalonians indicating the genuineness of their faith in Christ. The tense denotes a continuous action and thus the expression indicates that at all times and seasons of prayer thanksgiving was given to God for every one of the Thessalonian believers. Paul and his companions were swift to acknowledge the goodness of God, not only in blessing their labours but in enriching others. They were men of thanksgiving. The believer should be characterised by thanksgiving (Ephesians 5:20).

"making mention of you in our prayers:" The deep interest in those who had been saved through their labours - that they may be kept in the midst of persecution and grow in the things of God. The result of a deep desire for their well being and spiritual development. We should have this desire for our fellow believers.

Verse 3. **"Remembering without ceasing"** The calling to mind of something. The idea here is of a constantly recurring remembrance on every occasion of prayer - consistency in prayer and thanksgiving (see 2:13; 5:17). The remembrance here is of the three Christian graces, faith, love and hope, which were evident in these Thessalonian believers.

"your" This word is placed at the head of the three expressions but should be taken with all three. It emphasises what was characteristic of the Thessalonians.

"work of faith," The working reality of their faith. The course or conduct that springs from faith - work that had its roots in God. Faith is an operating principle of life or a working power in life. Faith without works is dead (James 2:20). Here we have the idea of origin which would indicate that the Christian life springs from faith or the idea of possession indicating the activity of faith.. Faith expresses itself in activity that is in keeping with the word of God. An illustration of this would be Abraham in the offering of Isaac (Heb 11:17-19).

"labour of love," The word 'labour' here denotes arduous labour - your toiling of love. Love being the stimulating force of wearying toil - toil being the expression of their love. The genuineness of their love was manifested in their toiling. Love is only known by its action - self-denying, self-sacrificing love which gives itself by toiling on the behalf of others. The idea is that of labour belonging to love and love characterising the labour. We see a picture of this in David's three mighty men who, out of love for David, risked their lives to bring him water from the well at Bethlehem (2Sam 23:13-17). The motive of all true Christian activity is love.

"patience of hope" The steadfast endurance of hope - enduring under pressure. It is not a passive patience or endurance but has the ides of being unswerving in the will of God and being unmoved by the greatest opposition because of the hope of a future day. Their patience was inspired by hope and hope characterised the patience. When we have our minds and affections set on things above and on the Lord's coming we will endure in the pathway of the will of God which is unfolded in His word. This is illustrated in in Gen 24:61-67 - Rebekah enduring the journey by camel in anticipation of being joined to Isaac.

"in our Lord Jesus Christ," The thought here is of the hope of the coming of our Lord Jesus Christ. The Lord's coming is the hope of every child of God and should be the stimulating force in order to endure with joy in the Christian pathway.

Their faith motivated their activity, love in their hearts motivated their toil and the assurance of the Lord's coming enabled them to endure the hardships of the way. Faith was displayed in their works, love spent itself for others and hope patiently waited for the Lord's coming.

"in the sight of God and our Father" Before, or in, the presence of God and our Father. This is linked with verse 2 and the first words of this verse - remembering without ceasing before God and our Father.

Verse 4. **"Knowing, brethren beloved, your election of God."** - or knowing brethren, beloved of God, your election. Here is a knowledge obtained by observation. The lives of the Thessalonian believers demonstrated that their faith was genuine. They were brethren, indicating relationship based upon origin, possessing the same life and in the same family. 'Brethren' is not a denominational name but a name that applies to every genuine believer in Christ. Sad to say this term is often used in an unscriptural way and imply that the assemblies constitute a denomination which is not true. They were loved ones of God - the tense indicates loved and being loved of God. Oh that we might constantly be in the enjoyment of that love. Their election was demonstrated by their lives - known only after their faith in Christ. We can link verses 2 & 4 "Giving thanks ..... since we know ......" - or verses 3 & 4 "Remembering .... since we know ....".

Verses 5-7 The Entrance of the Gospel into Thessalonica
We can look at these verses under six headings.

(1) The Preaching of the Gospel
Verse 5. **"For"** Or since - the ground of thanksgiving mentioned in verse 2.

"our gospel" The message they brought and proclaimed. Here we have the servants' responsibility to proclaim the message committed to them. This message is called the 'gospel of God' (2:2) indicating its origin and 'the gospel of Christ' indicating its subject and substance.

"came not unto you in word only," Yes it came with words but not just words to occupy the time - not merely a statement of facts or sermonising. It was not just an interesting discourse. It came with words that conveyed a definite and distinct message containing the truth of God.

<u>(2) The Power of the Gospel</u>
"but also in power," The Greek word translated 'power' is the word from which we get our English words dynamic and dynamite. This is power in utterance. This is the inherent power of the gospel by virtue of its nature - living. It was not intellectual or plausible, because of human reasoning, but that which contained power to convict and illuminate.

"in the Holy Ghost," It came in power but that power was the power of the Holy Spirit thus the thought is 'in Holy Spirit power'. The power of the gospel was that convicting and illuminating power that demonstrated the work of the Spirit of God. The transforming power of the gospel reveals the sovereign work of the gracious Spirit of God. Just as dynamite is harmless unless ignited so the preaching of the gospel without the working of the Spirit of God will never produce conviction and salvation.

<u>(3) The Presentation of the Gospel</u>
"in much assurance:" In certain or absolute assurance. The word here is only used on three other occasions in the New Testament. On those occasions it is translated "full assurance" In Col 2:2 it is linked with love, in Heb 6:11 it is linked with hope and in Heb 10:22 it is linked with faith.. Some link the statement with the servants and others with the Thessalonians. We embrace both. The servants, fully assured of the truth of the gospel, confidently and with liberty, proclaimed its message so that the Thessalonians were fully assured that it came from God. The gospel should always be proclaimed with conviction, conveying to the listeners that it is the message of God to them. It is the only message that will meet the need of guilty sinners.

<u>(4) The Proof of the Gospel</u>
"as ye know" A knowledge through observation - they had witnessed these facts -they had watched and witnessed the behaviour of the servants.

"what manner of men we were among you" What we became or proved to be. The Thessalonians were witnesses to the fact that the servants behaved in keeping with the message they proclaimed. Their preaching and behaviour enhanced the message they declared. The proof of the gospel was the servants themselves - their preaching, conduct and demeanour. They practised what they preached - "How beautiful are the feet (not lips) of them that preach the gospel of peace" (Rom 10:15). How important in testimony is the life of the child of God - "let your conversation be as it becometh the gospel of Christ" (Phil 1:27) - let your manner of life be in keeping with the message you claim to believe and which you proclaim. A consistent godly life is a powerful testimony to the truth of the gospel.

"for your sake." One of the reasons for such preaching and behaviour was that the truth of the gospel might have its affect upon the Thessalonians. The servants were careful not to mar the presentation of the gospel but to conduct themselves in keeping with the message for the benefit of the Thessalonians. God enabled the servants and the servants so preached and lived that the result was the salvation of these Thessalonians. This is surely a voice to all who proclaim the gospel.

(5) The Purpose of the Gospel
Verse 6. **"ye became followers"** - imitators. The tense either looks back to that moment when they trusted Christ or suggests the whole life or purpose of the change that had taken place, i.e. what they became in their Christian life.. The verb form is found in the continuous tense in 2Thess 3:7, 9 indicating that there is to be a continuous or constant following or imitating.

"Of us, and of the Lord," They had been brought into contact with the Perfect Pattern through the servants who were models of the Christian life. The Lord had suffered in proclaiming and carrying out the will of God - so had the apostle and his companions - now these Thessalonian believers were experiencing the same. The Thessalonians had not only accepted the truth but copied the examples set before them. Not only had their destiny changed but also their lives and this is the purpose of the gospel. If there is no change in the life a question mark can be put over the reality of faith in Christ.

"having received" Having embraced as your own - a deliberate and willing acceptance. This reception had a two fold affect.

"in much affliction," The external affect of receiving the truth - what men did to them. The pressure caused by opposition - affliction because of persecution. The world is ever opposed to the truth of God and thus is against the people of God.

"with joy of the Holy Ghost:" The internal affect of receiving the truth - joy wrought by the Holy Spirit. Here we see inward joy and gladness in spite of the opposition and persecution. Joy is not joviality but an inward delight or gladness in the Lord and in the things of God whatever the circumstances.

(6) The Pattern they Set
Verse 7. **"So that ye were ensamples to all that believe in Macedonia and Achaia."** Ye became ensamples. The effect of the gospel on the lives of the Thessalonians was such that they became patterns for others to follow. The word 'ensamples' carries the idea of an impression, a type in printing or a pattern cut out. Their lives left an impression on others - they became a type to be printed out in the lives of other believers - they were patterns cut out for others to follow. How do we measure up to this? Would we like other believers to live as we live?

Verses 8-10 The Expansion of the Gospel
Verse 8. **"For"** How they were examples having received the truth of the gospel.

"from you sounded out" As a radio transmitter going or radiating out from the Thessalonians. The word translated 'sounded out' is only found here and carries the thought of a herald's trumpet - a loud unmistakable sound like thunder. They certainly made sure that all were aware of the change in their lives and what it was that had produced that change.

"the word of the Lord" The word which came from the Lord or the word concerning the Lord. The word that carried the authority of the Lord.

"not only in Macedonia and Achaia," Macedonia where Thessalonica was - Achaia where Paul was writing from.

"also in every place" The main places - carried along the main land and sea routes. Their testimony was carried over a wide area. The change in their lives and the reason for it became a subject of conversation everywhere. What about the testimony of the assembly in the locality where we live?

"your faith to God-ward is spread abroad:" The direction or object of their faith was God and this was continually evident to all. There was a consistent testimony to their lift of faith.

"we need not speak any thing." No need for the servants to speak of the effect of the gospel in Thessalonica for this was evident in the lives and testimony of the Thessalonian believers.

Verse 9. **" For they themselves ....entering in .....unto you,"** All were aware of that which the gospel had wrought in Thessalonica. The change in the lives of these believers and the character of their faith was common knowledge. The result of the entrance of the gospel into Thessalonica was reported over a wide area.

"and how" The continued subject of the wide spread report - the reason for the change in the Thessalonian believers.

"ye turned" Conversion - a right about turn. The tense indicates a once for all action - an immediate and decisive change having twofold result. Conversion is linked both to faith and to repentance (Acts 11:21; 26:20).

"to God" Positive - once facing away from God but now facing towards God. The preposition indicates movement as well as direction - towards God. The primary idea seems one of being acceptable to God, sin having been dealt with, and the enjoyment of fellowship with God. The secondary idea is that of an increasing enjoyment of fellowship with God who not only saves but satisfies. Every believer should have an increasing enjoyment of fellowship with God.

"from idols" Again the preposition indicates movement as well as direction - away from idols. The primary idea seems to be that of being severed from what they were in their sins. The secondary idea would be that of moving away from the old manner of life - away from anything and everything that would hinder or mar the enjoyment of fellowship with God - away from all that would come between the heart's affection and Christ. The old manner of life set aside, left behind - practically, experimentally - in our lives day by day.

"to serve" The idea is that of serving as a bond servant - as one who has been purchased and who has his master's interests at heart. We have been bought with a price and thus our desire should be to serve Christ faithfully and devotedly. His will should be paramount, His word should be adhered to and His interests should be ours. The Christian should live a life of obedience to the will and word of God.

"the living and true God:" Here the character of God is emphasised. He is living, in contrast to the lifeless idols and as the One who is the source of all life. He is true, genuine, in contrast to the false gods and as the One who is the source of all that is true. He alone fulfils the designation God.

Verse 10. **"to wait"** The word is only found here and has the idea of waiting with a patient and confident expectancy. The tense indicates to keep on waiting. It is not a passive waiting but is active - not content that they are ready but serving the interests of the God who saved them. They were serving the One for whom they were waiting and desiring that others might be ready for His coming.

"for his Son" The Son of the living and true God. It is the Son who we wait for, the One who loved us and gave Himself for us. He has promised to come and will fulfil that promise.

"from heaven," Out of heaven - the place where He is now. An indication of His ascension and exaltation.

"whom he raised from the dead," From among the dead

indicating His presidency in resurrection - "the firstfruits of them that slept" (1 Cor 15:20) and the firstborn from the dead" (Col 1:18). The proof of a finished work.

"even Jesus," Emphasises His manhood - the despised One - the One who once moved in this scene. We note that none of the disciples ever addressed Him by this Name alone.

"which delivered us" The One who delivereth us or the delivering One. Here the thought is not of a past deliverance but of a future deliverance. Thus He is not only the Coming One but also the Delivering One. The verb translated 'delivered' carries the thought of rescuing by drawing to one's self - to rescue from coming danger by drawing to one's self.

"from the wrath to come." Away from the coming wrath. The preposition indicates away from the face of coming wrath. The coming wrath has reference to the judgment to be poured out upon this world. The indication here is that the Lord Jesus, the coming One, the delivering One, will rescue His own, by drawing them to Himself, away from the face of the wrath coming upon this world. The Church will not go through the tribulation - "we are not appointed unto wrath, but to obtain salvation by our Lord Jesus Christ" (1 Thess 5:9).

The Lord's coming here seems to be linked with salvation indicating that the imminent return of Christ is the immediate hope of every believer and should have a powerful effect upon the life. Appreciation of this thrilling fact will deliver us from apathy and indifference.

How the Servants Conducted Themselves

In this chapter the apostle rehearses how he and his companions entering into Thessalonica (Verses 1-12), tells of their thanksgiving for the Thessalonians' reception of the gospel and their steadfastness in persecution (Verses 13-16) and then unfolds his desire to see them (Verses 17-20). The chapter can be divided into these three sections:- Verses 1-12 The Preachers of the Word, Verses 13-16 The Persecution of the Saints and Verses 17-20 The Purpose of Paul. The first two sections are linked with chapter 1:9.

Verses 1-12 The Preachers of the Word
This section can be divided into two parts:- Verses 1-6 The Coming of the Servants and Verses 7-12 The Care and Manner of the Preachers.

1. Verses 1-6 The Coming of the Servants
Verse1. **"For"** A reference back to 1:5. That which was stated there is now further developed. There is also a link with 1:9 for what others reported the Thessalonians knew to be true.

"yourselves, brethren, know our entrance in unto you," Although some feel it should read "they themselves" referring it to the believers in Macedonia and Achaia (1:8-9) we believe the reference is to the experience and knowledge of the Thessalonians. The apostle first draws attention to the Thessalonians' knowledge of their coming to Thessalonica with the gospel and to their relationship with him - 'for you yourselves know, brethren'. We notice five things about that coming:-

<u>(1) Their Coming was Purposeful</u>
"not in vain:" Not empty - not fruitless - not hollow as to content

- not empty or lacking in purpose and earnestness. Their coming with the truth of the gospel was in order to produce something for God in Thessalonica. The idea seems to be that of the earnest desire of the servants to leave behind them in Thessalonica continuing and lasting results for the glory of God. There was no desire for mere empty profession. They had come with a definite purpose and thus they did not waste time in aimless pursuits but went out to the people with the gospel. The character of their preaching is really in view. The tense indicates the lasting effects of the preaching in Thessalonica. How do we preach? Is it with real earnestness, wanting to see something for God, or simply out of a sense of duty?

<u>(2) Their Coming was with Courage</u>
Verse 2. **"even after that we had suffered . . . Philippi,"** A reference to their previous suffering recorded in Acts 16. 'Shamefully entreated' has the idea of insulting and outrageous treatment calculated to publicly insult and humiliate them. It was not only physical but also mental suffering. Such treatment would deter many from making known the Gospel. The world is always opposed to the Gospel and would seek to silence those who would proclaim its message. The persecution had not dampened their spirits or discouraged them but actually had the opposite affect upon them. Yet often we who suffer little or no persecution today have not the same zeal or courage.

"we were bold in our God" They were undaunted and spoke freely the message committed to them. They continued in the work without fear, for their confidence was in God. They were courageous in God and not in themselves and thus they depended upon God for protection and help in their preaching. We should never allow opposition to prevent us from serving God, or living for God, for our sufficiency is found in Him, and in Him alone. One has said that courage is not fear absent but fear conquered.

"to speak unto you the gospel of God" They were bold in making known the truth of God, the glad tidings of salvation. They courageously proclaimed the message of God despite past suffering and present conflict. It was the message that God had given them to proclaim - they had the responsibility of making known this message to their fellow men. Thus they faithfully and boldly made it known to the Thessalonians. How do we face up to our responsibilities to carrying out and maintaining the things of God? Are we faithful in the handling of divine truth?

"with much contention." Conflict - the Greek word is translated 'conflict' in Phil 1:30; Col 2:1, 'fight' in 1 Tim 6:12; 2 Tim 4:7 and 'race' in Heb 12:1. Here it indicates the difficulties and hardships experienced at Thessalonica. It is more than likely a reference to the opposition of the Jews (Acts 17:5-9). With courage they came to Thessalonica to proclaim the gospel of God and did not cease to make it known when face with opposition. This indicates the intense effort of the servants in their preaching in spite of strong opposition. How do we react to opposition, to the sneer, to the laughter or the scorn? It is not easy to go on for God in the face of opposition but, by His grace, it is possible to continue for Him. Often opposition produces faithfulness and strength of character with regard to the things of God.

(3) Their Coming was with Purity
Verse 3 **"For"** The apostle now combats the false charges made against them by stating their integrity and faithfulness. How often have the servants of God, down the centuries been slandered by those opposed to them and to the message of God they proclaim.

"our exhortation" Our appeal. This refers to the whole course of their labours and indicates that they had the Thessalonians at heart. Thus both exhortation and consolation are embraced in the word. It is the urging of behaviour suitable to those who had trusted Christ and consolation in view of the opposition. The servants had a deep conviction that the message they proclaimed was the very message that would meet the need of the Thessalonians. It is the gospel message that will meet the need of men today and it is wholesome teaching of the Word of God that will meet the need of the saints today.

"not of deceit," Not of (out of) error - it wasn't false, it wasn't a fable. The servants had not been carried away by error nor had they sought to mislead others in their preaching. The message was not calculated to lead astray but was the truth which would bring blessing to them. It was genuine, being the unadulterated word of God, in contrast to the deceit Paul warned them against (2 Thess 2:5). This was why they were bold in their preaching. They had complete faith and trust in the Word of God. Do we?

"nor uncleanness," They did not gratify the flesh. The idea seems to be that of being free from either lust for power or greed for gain. The servants were free from self-ambition, self-advancement and desires for pleasing themselves. This was in complete opposition to the spirit of the world and still is today. The servants' motives were pure. The word is used relative to the ungodly in Rom 1:24. We also note that error and impurity are associated (2Pet 2:18; Jude 4) thus there is the thought of holiness of life. We see that personal holiness is demanded in the Christian life and is essential in the service of God.

"nor in guile." A cloak covering over one's motives. The idea is that of a bait to ensnare and thus to deceive. They did not use deceit or craft to take advantage of the Thessalonians. They had come to Thessalonica not for themselves but for the benefit of the Thessalonians. The source of their message was the God of truth, they had the Thessalonians' well being at heart and they used the right method to bring them blessing.

Paul is saying - our message was true, our motives were pure, our conduct was blameless and our lives were transparent. How important these things are in the lives of all the saints today.

(4) Their Coming was of God
Verse 4. **"as"** - so as, just as or according as.

"we were allowed of God" The word translated 'allowed' has the idea of proved or approved. The thought here is of being approved by God - approved by testing. One has suggested that this was the seal of God upon them in regard to their labours. The tense here indicates a lasting approval. This is the reason for their faithfulness.

"to be put in trust with the gospel," To be entrusted with the gospel - here we see the result of being approved by God. Having been divinely tested and having received divine approval they were then entrusted with the Gospel (1 Tim 1:12). Heaven's approval is so vital in Christian life and service. They did not choose this ministry but were chosen for it. We too must seek to determine what the Lord wants us to do for Him - we all have a part to play in the service of God. However, we must recognise that we will be put to the test as to our trustworthiness in handling of the things of God.

"even so we speak;" They spoke as those approved by God and entrusted with the gospel. They were deeply conscious of their responsibility and so proclaimed faithfully that message entrusted to them by God. The message is not the servant's to change in any way but to communicate faithfully - "it is required in stewards, that a man be found faithful" (1 Cor 4:2).

"not as pleasing men, but God," The purpose of their preaching was not to please men (Gal 1:10). The gospel message is not palatable to men but it rather condemns men. They ever sought, in their preaching, to please God whose servants they were, and who had entrusted them with the gospel. The thought here is of striving to please by faithfully and obediently serving the One who had entrusted this service to them. Are we seeking to please God in our lives and service? What do we seek to do in our preaching or teaching - simply to please men or are we faithful in our proclamation and thus pleasing God?

"which trieth our hearts." Another reason for their faithfulness and integrity. The word translated 'trieth' is the same word translated 'allowed' in this verse - to prove or approve after putting to the test. Here it has to do with the thoughts and intents of the heart. They were deeply conscious that God would put to the test the motives behind their preaching. God will put all that we do, think and say to the test as well as try the motives of our hearts. Everything is open before the eyes of the Lord (Heb 4:13). He alone knows the true motives of our hearts. How solemn, how searching. Are we daily conscious of this solemn fact?

(5) Their Coming was not for Themselves

Verse 5. **"For"** The development of the last part of verse 4. In the former verses Paul has asserted their integrity in a general way but now he deals with particular aspects of their coming to them.

"neither at any time used we flattering words," The expression 'flattering words' is only found here in the New Testament. It means words to flatter in order to please men and thus further the flatterer's own interests. It means making the message palatable and readily acceptable to men so that the preachers themselves would benefit. The servants were not guilty of this, for they knew full well that the gospel never flatters or soothes but must expose and convict, before bringing peace to those who repent and trust Christ. How many have either withheld truth or changed or watered it down in order to please men (see Isaiah 30:10; 2 Tim 4:3). How important it is for the servant to communicate all the truth of God, however unpalatable it may seem at the time.

"as ye know," The Thessalonians had heard and experienced their preaching and thus Paul appeals to them as witnesses of this fact. Flattering words could be discerned and generally men love to be flattered. The servants had shown they were genuine in their preaching. Are we faithful and forthright in our preaching?

"nor a cloak of covetousness;" Not a covering over of their intention to make gain from their preaching. The servants were not out to further their own selfish interest at the expense of the Thessalonians. They were not seeking to exploit their hearers in order to enrich themselves. Since they were not marked by covetousness they had no need of a cloak. We need to be transparent as the people of God with no need to cover over things.

"God is witness:" Here is a solemn appeal to God (Rom 1:9; 2 Cor 1:23; Phil 1:8). What the Thessalonians could not know God knew. God was a witness to the intents and desires of their hearts.

Thus there was a twofold witness to the fact that they spoke as from God and before God and neither flattered men or sought personal gain - the Thessalonians themselves and the all-knowing God.

Verse 6. **"Nor of men sought we glory,"** This means honour or praise which is in fact the opposite to humility. Unlike the Pharisees (John 5:44) they did not seek honour or praise of men . They had no desire to be set on a pedestal by anyone. Although honour, dignity or praise seems the main thought here, there could also be the idea of material gain in the word 'glory'. The servants had not even sought material support from the Thessalonians.

"neither of you, nor of others," They did not seek anything from the Thessalonian believers nor from other saints. How do we measure up to this? There is the desire in the human breast to desire honour and the praise of others but we must resist this in the service of God.

"when we might have been burdensome, as the apostles of Christ." 'Burdensome' carries the idea of a weight of authority and is linked with the word 'glory'. Although as the apostles of Christ, sent by the sovereign Lord, dignity and honour did belong to them, they never sought honour from men, not even from the saints. Neither did they seek material support. They never stood upon that dignity that was theirs nor made a claim of honour. They never demanded place or material support and they never put themselves on a pedestal as the servants of Christ. We should all question our hearts in this matter. Why are we engaged in Christian service? Do we seek position, praise or honour from men? We should be constantly on our guard against pride in our service for God. Even when standing for the truth or proclaiming the truth the motive can be wrong.

2. Verses 7-12 The Care of the Servants

Having dealt with the negative side and the charges made against them by their enemies, the apostle now turns to the positive side and describes their behaviour among the saints. We can look at these verses under two headings:- Verses 7-9 The Tenderness of a Mother and Verses 10-12 The Faithfulness of a Father.

(1) Verses 7-9 The Tenderness of a Mother

Verse 7 Their Loving Care. **"we were gentle among you,"** Gentle here has the thought of tender - handling carefully so as not to harm. This is seen in perfection in Christ (Isaiah 40:11; 42:3). This is opposite to flattery. Their conduct was that which was required of the servants of the Lord (2 Tim 2:24) and which should characterise every child of God today.

"even as a nurse cherisheth her children" As a nursing mother cherishes her own children. 'Cherisheth' means to warm, to nourish by taking to the bosom - to look after with special care. This word is only found elsewhere in Eph 5:29 "For no man ever yet hated his own flesh; but nourisheth and cherisheth it, even as the Lord the church:" Thus their care was selfless and sacrificial. We should act towards our fellow believers as we would act towards ourselves and as the Lord acts towards the church. The standard is high but we dare not lower it. The word is found in the Greek Old Testament of a bird sitting upon her young or upon her eggs (Deut 22:6) - the idea is of warmth and protection.

Verse 8 Their Longing or Love. **"So being affectionately desirous of you,"** Having a strong affection for them and a deep longing for their welfare. It was the Thessalonians they longed for and not material things. An attraction to them and an affection for them. It was like the deep longing of a mother for the well being of her children whom she loves, which is shown by the next expression.

"We were willing to have imparted unto you," What they did they did willingly not out of necessity. As a mother acts towards her own children so they acted toward the Thessalonians who were their spiritual children. They had a deep desire to impart to them that which would be of benefit to them just as a mother longs to benefit her children who are so dear to her (see Rom 1:11; Gal 4:19). Oh that we had this deep longing for the spiritual well being of our fellow believers.

"Not the gospel of God only, but also our own souls," Yes the servants were prepared to impart the gospel to them but they were also prepared to impart their souls to the Thessalonians. They were willing to hazard their lives for them. They were prepared to spend their lives on their behalf - to give their all which was a proof of their love - "Hereby perceive we the love of God. Because he laid down his life for us: and we ought to lay down our lives for the brethren." (1 John 3:16). What about us? This is not really a choice but an obligation for every child of God.

"because ye were dear unto us." Literally became beloved of us - that love was there at first but increased and developed. Their love was the basis of their labour. The saints were so dear to them that they would have laid down their lives for them. How dear are the saints to us? How far are we prepared to go for the benefit of fellow believers?

Verse 9 Their Labour. **"For ye remember, brethren,"** Again the apostle calls them to remember and uses a note of tenderness and affection. The Thessalonians could not but remember the labours of Paul and his companions, working to support themselves and preaching the gospel.

"Our labour and travail:" Their wearying toil and struggle to overcome difficulties and opposition to bring the gospel to them and to see them established in the Christian faith. There is always a cost to be paid in faithful service for God. There are difficulties to be overcome and opposition to be faced when seeking to live for God. We must remember we are in a warfare daily and that we must redeem the time, because the days are evil (Eph 5:16).

"Labouring night and day," A constant and continual labour that was fatiguing. Working to the point of exhaustion and struggling against hardships. This included toiling with their hands to supply for their physical needs - constantly active in either physical or spiritual labour. How like a mother expending herself for the welfare of her children (see 1 Thess 3:10).

"Because we would not be chargeable unto any of you," The end in view. They would not make demands upon the Thessalonians in order that their needs might be met (2 Thess 3:8). They were not there to be a burden to the Thessalonians. They did not seek or demand support from the Thessalonians which was another proof of their love. Just as a mother gives all and demands nothing from her children who are dear to her, so the servants gave themselves demanding nothing in return. The believer should ever be self-less in seeking to be a help to others.

"We preached unto you the gospel of God." Freely and diligently proclaiming the glad tidings from God to them. The threefold ministry of Evangelist, Shepherd and Teachers seem to be mentioned in this first section.

(2) Verses 10-12 The Faithfulness of a Father
Verse 10 Their Example. **"Ye are witnesses, and God also,"** The apostle now declares that both the Thessalonian believers and God were witnesses to their conduct and care. Whatever others might have thought there was a twofold witness to their behaviour while in Thessalonica.

"How holily" - piously. This can be viewed as Godward. They conducted themselves as those who were set apart to and for God. They were marked by holiness of life because of purity within. They were free from the impurity that characterised those opposed to them. This is the witness of God to their purity of mind and life. Holiness of life springs from purity within.

"and justly" - righteously. This can be viewed as manward. They acted in a right way towards men as before God. This is the witness of men to their righteous actions. The inevitable consequences of holiness.

"and unblameably" This can be viewed as self-ward. Without cause for reproach - i.e. no charge could be justly laid upon them for either acting contrary to the character of God or unjustly towards men. This is the witness of their own consciences.

The servants were examples to the saints in the same way as a father should be to his children. Every elder should be such an example to the saints and every believer should be such an example to fellow believers.

"we behaved ourselves among you that believe:" Their deportment at Thessalonica and particularly among the saints.

Verses 11 Their Entreaty. **"As ye know how we exhorted"** Here we have an appeal or exhortation to a particular line of conduct. A strong entreaty to them to conduct themselves as becoming the children of God. We see the earnestness of the servants.

"and comforted" To encourage or persuade them as to a certain course. They encouraged by giving an incentive. The saints needed encouragement in the midst of persecution. In this we see the thoughtfulness of the servants. How do we seek to encourage the saints - particularly those we know are going through difficult times?

"and charged" A solemn injunction or witness. Here we see the seriousness of the servants.

"every one of you," Applicable to every one of the Thessalonian believers. There was no exception to their exhortation, encouragement and charge.

"as a father doth his children," The figure of a mother emphasises the tenderness of love whereas the figure of a father has in view the firmness of that same love.

Verse 12 The Reason. The contents of the charge mentioned in verse 11.

"That ye should walk worthy of God," The word translated 'worthy' is found five more times in the New Testament:- (i) Rom 16:2 "That ye receive her in the Lord, as <u>becometh</u> saints," - worthily of saints - in keeping with those who bear the name of saints; (ii) Eph 4:1 "walk <u>worthy</u> of the vocation wherewith ye are called" - worthily of your calling - in keeping with your calling; (iii) Phil 1:27 "Only let your conversation be as it <u>becometh</u> the gospel of Christ:" - worthily of the gospel - in keeping with the message you received and proclaim; (iv) Col 1:10 "That ye might walk <u>worthy</u> of the Lord" - worthily of the Lord - in keeping with the claims of the Lord; (v) 3 John 6 "whom if thou bring forward on their journey <u>after</u> a godly sort" - worthily of God - in a way that reflects the care and character of God. Here in 1 Thess 2:12 the thought is that of living in keeping with the will and character of God - living as those who are the people of God (1 Pet 1:15-16).

"who hath called you unto his kingdom and glory." We see from Acts 17:7 that the servants had preached about the kingdom of God and the Lord as King. Because God has called us unto His kingdom, which will be manifested in a coming day, and because He has called us to partake of His glory, we ought to live worthily of Him (see 1 Pet 5:10). The present continuous tense here suggests that God has called and continues to call unto His kingdom and glory - this is a continual incentive to live in keeping with the will and word of God and to make spiritual progress. Let us all seek to make progress in our Christian lives day by day until He comes or calls us to Himself.

Verses 13-16 The Persecution of the Saints
(1) Verse 13 The Reception of the Word
"For this cause also thank we God without ceasing," In this verse the apostle gives another reason for the servants' constant thanksgiving to God which was mentioned at the beginning of the epistle. The word 'also' would indicate that the Thessalonians as well as the servants were thankful to God for their reception of the gospel. Believers should always be thankful (Eph 5:20).

"Because, when ye received the word of God which ye heard of us," They heard the message, took heed to it and received it (Rom 10:17). There are two Greek words translated 'received' in this verse. The word 'received' here has the idea of a formal receiving as the receiving of tradition - the receiving with the ear as to facts.

"ye received it not as the word of men," The word 'received' here has the idea of welcoming or believing. Not only had they received the message but they had welcomed or accepted it, but not as the message of men. Yes, men brought the message to them but they were but messengers, they were not the source of the message.

"but as it is in truth, the word of God," The message they had welcomed had its source in God and came from Him. The message proceeded from God who was its Author. The power of the Spirit of God brought the gospel home to the conscience as the message of God to them and as such they had embraced it. How do we receive the teaching of the Word of God? As the truth of God to be adhered to or as something that we can ignore?

"which effectually worketh also in you that believe." Worketh now means worketh presently in you. 'Effectually' is to work efficiently and productively (Eph 1:19; Phil 2:13). We have a reference here to the continuing power of the gracious Spirit of God, working through the Word of God in their lives - the practical effect of the message they embraced in their lives. This was the cause of the servants' thanksgiving. If the Word of God doesn't affect the life there is something drastically wrong. Knowledge of the Word of God is valueless unless it affects the life. Sadly it is possible to have a knowledge of the word of God and yet for this knowledge to have little effect on the way we live our lives.

(2) Verse 14 The Result of Salvation
"For ye, brethren" Again notice the term of endearment or relationship because they accepted the Word of God.

"became followers of the churches of God" As an assembly of God they became followers of assemblies in Judea which had been established earlier. Note the plurality of assemblies in Judea indicating fellowship between assemblies but no central government of assemblies - each assembly is directly responsible to the Lord and responsible for maintaining a collective testimony to all the truth of God in the locality in which it has been placed. In receiving the gospel the Thessalonians became followers or imitators of the believers in Judea in the sense of suffering reproach and persecution (Acts 17). The result of receiving the gospel was the same everywhere - opposition, persecution, suffering. "Yea, and all that will live godly in Christ Jesus shall suffer persecution." (2Tim 3:12) - there is still opposition today for those who allow the Word of God to affect their lives. Godliness will bring resentment from the world and, sad to say, from carnal believers. The winds of persecution soon remove the chaff and reveal loyalty of heart. We must be prepared to suffer for His sake.

"which in Judea are in Christ Jesus:" They became followers of what had taken place in Judea - followers in the same blessings, in the same responsibilities but particularly in suffering. There may be a reference to suffering in the same way as the believers in Judea (see Heb 10:32-34). This was not strange since they were followers of the One who was despised and rejected (see 1Pet 4:12-13). We note that just as the persecution in Judea had not stamped out the assemblies there or prevented the spread of the gospel, so persecution in Thessalonica had not annihilated the assembly there or hindered the spiritual progress of the saints. We must not allow persecution to hinder spiritual growth.

"for ye also have suffered like things of your own countrymen," The Jews stirred up the Gentiles so that the saints suffered at the hands of fellow Gentiles. Acts 17 shows how soon the storm of persecution burst upon them. They were fellow sufferers with the saints in Judea. They too were suffering at the hands of their own fellow nationals.

"even as they have of the Jews:" The believers in Judea had also suffered from their own countrymen. (The opposition of men to God and His purposes seen in the nation of Israel).

(3) Verses 15-16 The Reason for Persecution
Verse 15. **"Who both killed the Lord Jesus,"** The pinnacle or climax of the Jews opposition seen in the crucifixion of the Lord Jesus Christ (Matt 21:38; Acts 2:23; 3:14-15; 7:52).

"their own prophets," Their opposition did not commence at the advent of Christ but had been evident throughout their history. They had the same spirit as those of their nation who had slain the prophets. This spirit descended from one generation to another - they were their children (Matt 23:31, 37). This opposition was not just because of the new message but because of their hatred of reproof and their enmity to holiness. Opposition to God and His Word produces antagonism to the people of God.

"have persecuted us;" What they did to the Lord, they continued to do to His messengers. The word 'persecuted' has the idea of casting or driving out - pursued from place to place - caused to flee from one city to the next (see Acts 17:10, 13-14). This was well known to the Thessalonians.

"they please not God," The idea is that they greatly displeased God by their continued rebellion and rejection of His Word sent to them. They were opposed to God, The Law given by God, His prophets and now the gospel. Thus Israel was set aside by God.

"are contrary to all men:" Contrary not only to Christians but to all. Contrary in their despising of all other nations, in their religious principles and in hindering the spread of the gospel.

Verse 16. **"Forbidding us to speak to the Gentiles"** Israel is still in view in its opposition to God. They were opposed to the preaching of the gospel, not only to their own nation, but also to the Gentiles (Luke 4:28; Acts 22:21-22). They sought to forbid the preaching of the gospel by stirring up opposition (Acts 17:6).

"that they might be saved," This was the purpose of proclaiming the message to the Gentiles. Israel not only refused the gospel but they also, in their rebellion, sought to prevent others hearing and receiving it. This is also seen in Matt 23:13 - "Woe unto you Scribes and Pharisees, hypocrites, for ye shut up the kingdom of heaven against men: for ye neither go in yourselves, neither suffer ye them that are entering to go in". How dreadful it is to hinder anyone from hearing the gospel and to try to prevent anyone from trusting Christ.

"to fill up their sins alway:" In doing this they were filling up their history of sin and rebellion through their rejection and treatment of Christ and His apostles. They were causing their sins to rise up to the point of judgment (see Gen 15:16). God had borne with them down the centuries until this point (Matt 23:32). In His longsuffering God allows men to continue in their sin, giving them an opportunity to repent and receive His offer of salvation, but there comes a time when judgment is inevitable.

"for the wrath is come upon them to the uttermost." The judgment of God came upon the nation because of their continued rejection and rebellion. We can link this back to Chapter 1:10. Many feel that this is a reference to the invasion of Titus in 70 AD. However that was but the commencement of their judgement and a small picture of the final day of wrath (Jer 30:7; Matt 24:21-28). The continued rejection of the gospel and refusal of Christ in a person's life simply fills up the life of sin and ultimately brings the judgment of God upon that person.

Verses 17-20 The Purpose of the Servants
(1) Verse 17 The Heart's Desire Verse 17 follows quite naturally verse 12 so that verses 13-16 seems to be in parenthesis. Paul uses expressions in verse 17 to continue the idea of parents and children in contrast with verses 13-16.

"But we, brethren," Notice again the term of endearment in contrast to the hatred of the previous verse and used now because Paul is going to show how dear they were to him.

"being taken from you for a short time" The word 'taken', which only occurs here, has the idea of being bereaved or orphaned. It can be used of parentless children or childless parents - the separation was like that of parents torn away from their children. His leaving them was not voluntary but forced by persecution (Acts 17:10). It was as grievous to him as it was to them. He felt it as a father bereft of his children feels it. Do we feel separation from fellow believers like this? 'For a short time' is an idiom only found here in the New Testament and means for a brief interval or period. Paul had intended but a short separation from them. His longing was to be with them again in a short time but the time had become too long for him.

"in presence, not in heart," Separated in distance but not in affection. Separated in person but not in their thoughts. It was not the case of out of sight, out of mind. Love uniting them in spite of the distance. When we were saved we were brought into a sphere of love and we have a responsibility to love every child of God fervently (1 Pet 1:22)

"endeavouring the more abundantly to see your face" Exerting themselves exceedingly. This indicates the earnest effort of the apostle in trying to see them again.

"with great desire." Exceeding eagerness to see them because of his love for them. This indicates deep desire of the heart as in Phil 1:23 (see also Luke 22:15).

(2) Verse 18 The Hindrance of Satan
"Wherefore we would have come unto you," The word 'we' here seems to mean the servants in general and could refer to the intention of returning to Thessalonica from Berea..

"even I Paul, once and again;" Now Paul refers to himself particularly. Once, twice - these two words used together form an idiom, meaning more than once (see Phil 4:16). On at least two special occasions Paul had sought to visit Thessalonica to see them.

"but Satan hindered us." The word translated 'hindered' has the idea of cutting a trench or breaking up a road between one's self and an advancing army. It is to prevent or hinder reinforcements from relieving a siege. Satan thus hindered Paul returning to Thessalonica to be a help to the believers there. How he succeeded we do not know but it could have been by further persecution (see Acts 17:13-15) or by the bond that Jason had taken (see Acts 17:9). We know that he is always opposing the word, will and work of God. He hinders God's work of grace but we must appreciate that God allows Satan to hinder, yet often over rules in using the seeming hindrance to bring blessing to others. God is always in control and we must not forget this.

(3) Verses 19-20 The Hope of the Servants
Verse 19. **"For what is our hope,"** The reason for Paul's desire to see them again was the hope that they had not laboured in vain.

"joy" Gladness in their genuineness and in the fact that they were standing firm. Gladness in that coming day of review.

"Crown of rejoicing?" This means a victors crown of exulting - the evangelists crown (see also 1 Cor 9:24-27; 2 Tim 4:8; Jam 1:12; 1 Pet 5:4).

"Are not even ye" Here is the answer to Paul's question. The emphasis seems to be upon the Thessalonians being there as the fruit of His labours.

"in the presence of our Lord Jesus Christ at his coming?" It is important to see the construction of this phrase. The Greek word "emproethen" translated 'presence' has the idea of place or position and the Greek word "parousia" translated 'coming' has the thought of presence (W.E. Vine). Thus the whole expression would be "before our Lord Jesus Christ in his presence". The word "parousia" is not a point in time but rather a period of time which of necessity commences with a point in time and ends with a point in time. That period is the time of the Lord's presence with His own which commences at the rapture, includes introduction into the Father's house, the Judgment Seat and the marriage of the Lamb and ends with the revelation of Christ (see 2 Thess 2:8). Here the apostle has in mind the Judgment Seat when we will be before the Lord Jesus Christ and our lives and labours for Him will be reviewed. Paul is thinking of the Judgment Seat in relation to his labours at Thessalonica. Do we live with the Judgment seat of Christ before us? An appreciation of the imminent return of Christ will cause us to labour faithfully in view of the Judgment seat.

> *Only one life, yes only one;*
> *Soon will its fleeting hours be done;*
> *Then, in 'that day' our Lord to meet,*
> *And stand before His Judgment seat;*
> *Only one life, 'twill soon be past,*
> *Only what's done for Christ will last.*

"For ye are our glory and joy." In spite of the hindrance to his going to Thessalonica nothing could prevent him from exulting in them and being filled with joy, as he thought of that coming day. The day would dawn when all their labours will be over, the persecution would be past and Paul had no doubt that they would be reunited then. Paul could look forward to that day with joy knowing that he had faithfully served The Lord and that his labours were not in vain. As we examine our lives how do we look forward to that day of review?

CHAPTER 3

Where the Servants went and How they Acted

The chapter can be divided into three sections:- Verses 1-5 The apostle's concern for the saints; Verses 6-8 The apostle's comfort through the saints; and Verses 9-13 The apostle's constant prayer for the saints. In verses 1-5 we have Timothy's journey to Thessalonica brought before us, in verses 6-10 we have Timothy's return journey in view and in verses 11-13 we have Paul's intended journey to them.

Verses 1-5 The Apostle's Concern for the Saints

In this section we note four things in relation to the apostle- the deep longing he expressed - to know how they were faring; the desire he emphasises - to establish and comfort them; the difficulties he expected - afflictions and tribulation; and the danger he exposed - the possibility of them being moved by the tempter. Here we see in Paul the true characteristics of a father in the faith (see 2:11).

Verse 1. **"Wherefore"** That is in view of his great love for them and in light of the hindrances in his coming to them at Thessalonica. There is a link with verses 17-18 of chapter 2 which shows Paul's concern for the Thessalonians.

"when we" Although the plural form is used, Paul is referring to himself alone here (see also verse 5).

"could no longer forbear," The apostle continues to confirm his love and care for the Thessalonian saints by indicating his concern for them. The idea in the word 'forbear' is to endure the burden of being absent from them. His love and concern for

38

them was so great that he longed to be with them. Have we the same love and concern for our fellow believers? He says "we could no longer endure not knowing how you were faring there in Thessalonica". Paul's deep longing to know how things were in Thessalonica had to be satisfied and the strain on his mind had to be relieved

"we thought it good" The idea in the word translated 'good' is that of being willing, or willingly determined - what is pleasing as to his resolve of will - i.e. a deliberate choice. Only by the resolve of one's will can the believer carry out the will of God.

"to be left at Athens alone;" Although it would be a sore trial to be left alone in Athens the apostle was willing to be left there because he was so desirous of news about the Thessalonian believers. The expression 'left alone' carries the idea of being destitute of help. Paul would rather be destitute of help than have the saints in Thessalonica be destitute of help. He had greater consideration of them than of himself - thus we see the selflessness of the apostle. We are living in a day when the emphasis seems is upon self first which is opposite to the teaching of the Scriptures (Phil 2:4). Sad to say this spirit is often seen in Christians.

Verse 2. **"And sent Timotheus,"** Although Timothy's company and help was very desirable the apostle was willing to send him to Thessalonica to obtain news of the saints. We see the sacrificial love of Paul towards the saints.

"our brother," His relationship - the servants are seen here as being in the same family along with all the other saints. Being in the same family, believers are to be marked by fervent love one for another (1 Peter 1:22).

"and minister of God," Here we see his responsibility in rendering service to God. The Greek word used here is 'diakonos' which indicates a servant in relation to his work and thus indicates responsibility in carrying out that work. Every believer has a responsibility to be engaged in the work of God.

"and our fellowlabourer in the gospel of Christ," He was one who was engaged, along with others, in the work of making known the gospel. Paul acknowledges that Timothy laboured with him in the work of God which indicated Timothy's reliability.

"to establish you," To support or to strengthen you. The idea here seems to be that of placing a buttress in order to support something (see Exod 17:12). Here it is support for their faith in the face of persecution. Thus the thought of strengthening their faith, or establishing them firmly in their faith, through the ministry of Timothy.

"and to comfort you" The word translated 'comfort' has the idea of drawing alongside to aid, to help (as 2:11). The idea here is that of encouragement by exhortation and thus confirming their faith and comforting them in the midst of affliction and adversity. The ministry of the word of God is not only intended to instruct us as to the Divine Will but also to strengthen our faith and to encourage us in the things of God.

"concerning your faith:" Here we have faith and its confirmation, (in verse 5 we have faith and its conquest, in verse 6 we have faith and charity (love), in verse 7 we have faith and its comfort and in verse 10 we have faith and its completion). The word 'faith' can refer to the initial faith in Christ which brings salvation, to continuing faith in God and His word, or to the whole body of truth, the Word of God. One has suggested that all three would be involved in Timothy's work but the reference here seems to be in relation to their faith or trust in God and His word, in the midst of the persecution through which they were passing.

Verse 3. **"That no man should be moved"** The thought in the word 'moved' is that of being disturbed or shaken, in contrast to being firmly established in verse 2. There was a possibility of the saints being moved, disturbed or drawn away from the right path - from the hope of the gospel - by the persecution. There is a danger of being taken up with the afflictions that come our way and of allowing them to shake our faith and move us away from the will of God. Unexpected afflictions or opposition can shock and unsettle believers. How good to remember that in every circumstance God is still on the throne. Every child of God should stand firm in faith and not be moved away from the truth of God in the varying circumstances of life.

"by these afflictions:" The word 'afflictions' has the idea of pressure. It refers to anything that presses in on a person or anything that burdens the spirit. Here it seems to indicate the pressures of persecution. We note that the thought here is not that of being moved by affliction but being moved in their afflictions. They were actually going through severe persecution and the enemy sought to disturb them by these persecutions.

"for yourselves know" The apostle now reminds them of what they had already been informed.

"that we are appointed thereunto." The word translated "appointed" is translated 'set' in Phil 1:17 "set for the defence of the gospel" and in Matt 5:14 " a city set upon a hill". Here it indicates a situation in which one is placed. One has made the comment "this was their calling of God and thus they were destined for persecution." Suffering is not accidental but an essential part of the Christian life. Think of the following verses - "In me ye have peace. in the world ye shall have tribulation" (John 16:33) - "Beloved, think it not strange concerning the fiery trial which is to try you as though some strange thing happened unto you" (1 Peter 4:12). God often uses affliction for our benefit (Rom 5:3; 2 Cor 4:17). We ought to expect suffering while in this world and not be shaken by it when it comes. However, we must remember that suffering is not the ultimate destiny for the child of God but it is only temporary (1 Peter 1:6).

Verse 4. **"For verily, when we were with you,"** A reference to Acts 17. The Greek preposition translated 'with' implies an active intercourse which is borne out by the following statement.

"we told you before that we should suffer tribulation;" The apostle Paul had told the Thessalonians that persecution was the inevitable consequence of being children of God and thus they should expect to suffer persecution. The tense here indicates that the apostle repeatedly told them, so that they might not be taken unawares, by the persecution. Paul had learned this by experience as well as from the Old Testament Scriptures. The word translated 'tribulation' is closely associated with the word 'affliction' in verse 3 and means to suffer affliction, to be troubled, and refers to the pressures of the circumstances they were found in because of the antagonism of those opposed to the gospel. Paul not only told them of the blessings that came through faith in Christ but he also faithfully told them of the inevitable suffering that would follow. How important to teach young believers that not only joy and satisfaction of heart, but afflictions and trials are part of the Christian life.

"even as it came to pass, and ye know." What the apostle had forewarned them about they had now experienced. A reminder of this would be a source of strength to them, confirming that what Paul had proclaimed was indeed the truth.

Verse 5. **"For this cause,"** The persecution that had come upon the Thessalonian believers was the reason for the apostle's concern and for sending Timothy.

"when I could no longer forbear," A repetition of verse 1 emphasising his deep concern for them. Whereas in verse 1 it is linked with Paul's determination to send Timothy to strengthen and encourage them, here it is linked with his desire to know how they fared in the midst of the persecution.

"I sent to know your faith," We wanted to know if their faith had stood firm - to know how they were standing in the midst of persecution. Satan will always seek to weaken, undermine or destroy faith if he can. Thus we notice "concerning your faith" in verse 2 and "your faith" here. Faith is a vital link with God and if that is weakened then so is the believer. Paul had a deep concern for them and desired to know how they were managing. Timothy had not only been sent to be a help to the saints but also to obtain information for the apostle as to their Christian warfare.

Thus the verb translated 'know' (only found here in the epistle) has the idea of 'to get to know' or 'to ascertain'. How Paul longed to know of their spiritual condition. Have we the same concern for our fellow believers?

"lest by some means" By any means (see 2 Cor 11:3) - using any device possible.

"the tempter have tempted you," The expression 'the tempter, brings before us the character of the Devil. The Devil ever seeks to encourage men to act in a wrong way and to violate the word of God. The Devil was active in a two fold way :- a) active in hindering the return of the servants to Thessalonica (2:18) and b) seeking to intimidate the saints at Thessalonica through persecution and thus to undermine their faith. Today he is ever active in encouraging believers to neglect the things of God and to live for self. He seeks to undermine our faith and to encourage us in the things of the world. How we need to be on our guard against the cunning of the enemy as he seeks to rob us of spiritual progress and activity.

"and our labour be in vain." He did not want their labours, at Thessalonica, in proclaiming the gospel, to have been futile or fruitless. The idea here is that although the apostle thought that in all probability Satan had applied pressure on the believers in Thessalonica, he only thought it slightly possible that they had collapsed under the pressure. Paul fully expected that most, if not all, had stood firm, thus manifesting the reality of their faith in Christ. He was more concerned about their spiritual condition than their physical well being although he was not indifferent to their physical condition. We must ever remember that spiritual well being is more vital than physical or material well being.

Verses 6-8 The Apostle's Comfort through the Saints
Verse 6. **"But now when Timotheus came from you unto us,"** Paul now gives an account of Timothy's return and how he was affected by the news which he brought. The introduction of the word 'now' implies that this epistle was written on Timothy's

return from Thessalonica - "but Timotheus having just now come" (Alford).

"and brought us good tidings" This is the only occasion where the verb translated 'good tidings' is used, without it referring to the gospel. It means good news or glad tidings and this was certainly true of the report that Timothy had brought from Thessalonica - it was like water to a thirsty man. Two things brought Paul comfort, first their spiritual condition and then their remembrance of him.

"of your faith and charity," What a great comfort and encouragement it must have been to Paul to learn that the Thessalonians were going on in the things of God (see 3 John 4 - "I have no greater joy than to hear that my children walk in truth"). Their faith continued to be steadfast and it was expressed in love. The absence of 'hope' here could well signify their perplexity regarding some of their number who had passed on (The apostle deals with this in chapter 4).

"and that ye have good remembrance of us always," They had not forgotten the apostle who had brought the glad tidings to them even though he had been separated from them for some time. Elsewhere the word 'remembrance' is connected with prayer and that may be the thought here - they not only esteemed Paul and were grateful for his labours but they remembered the apostle in their prayers. Prayer unites believers in spite of separation.

"desiring greatly to see us," They not only remembered the apostle but they also longed for his presence with them once again - to see him and his fellow labourers.

"as we also to see you:" The apostle states that the longing was not one sided for he longed to be with them.

Verse 7. **"Therefore, brethren,"** Because of what he has already mentioned - the report of Timothy on his return.

"we were comforted over you" The news Timothy brought was a source of encouragement to the apostle. He had sent Timothy to comfort the Thessalonians, and now he is comforted by Timothy's report of them. The faithfulness and consistency of the saints was a great comfort to Paul. It is always an encouragement to see saints faithfully going on in the things of God. Are we giving encouragement to fellow believers in this way?

"in all our affliction and distress" The word translated 'affliction' is the same as verse 3 and 1:6 and may indicate here the pressure of hostility to him and his work for God. The word translated 'distress' carries the idea of necessity (1 Cor 9:16; Heb 7:12) which sometimes refers to a lack of material things (2 Cor 6:4) but which can indicate pressure upon the mind because of circumstances (Philemon 14). Hat his anxiety for the Thessalonian believers is not in view here because that would have been removed by the good news Timothy had brought. The events in Acts 18:5-17 may be in view here.

"by your faith:" The reason for his encouragement in the adverse circumstances.

Verse 8. **"For now we live,"** The concern of the apostle for the Thessalonians, exposed to such persecution so soon after trusting Christ, was so deep that he was like a man at the point of death. The news that Timothy brought was indeed like the gospel imparting new life to Paul, i.e. we live once more in spite of this distress and affliction. There are two ideas suggested:-
(i) It was life to the apostle to know that the Thessalonian believers were standing fast - failure of the work in Thessalonica would have been like a death blow to him. The good report, therefore, was like a new lease of life invigorating him. We are in full strength and freshness of life. (ii) He is implying that he lived to purpose in as much as the gospel was affective in them. Much of Paul's life was taken up with the spiritual well being of the assemblies as indicated in 2 Cor 11:28 "the care of all the churches" and thus he links his life with the assembly at Thessalonica.

"if ye stand fast in the Lord." There may be the suggestion that since Thessalonica was a strategic city Paul attached special importance to the work there. The preaching of the gospel elsewhere would be affected by their standing firm in the things of the Lord.

Verses 9-13 The Apostle's Constant Prayer for the Saints
Verse 9. **"For what thanks can we render to God again for you,"** Here is another effect of the news Timothy brought from Thessalonica. First Paul rejoiced at the news of the steadfastness of their faith and the inevitable reaction to that news was thanksgiving to God. The Greek word translated 'render' has the idea of recompense (2 Thess 1:6) or repayment (Rom 12:19) and is only used here of thanksgiving to God. In chapter 1:2-3 Paul's thanksgiving is in relation to their salvation, in chapter 2:13 it is in relation to the way they received the Word of God, but here it is for the joy that Timothy's report had brought to him. The apostle uses a question form to indicate that such was his joy at receiving the news that he was unable to give adequate thanksgiving to God. We will never be able to adequately give thanks to God for his Son or for all that He has bestowed upon us (Psalm 116:12). Are we constantly giving thanks to God for all His bounty bestowed upon us?

"for all the joy wherewith we joy for your sakes" The expression 'all the joy' does not refer to different kinds of joy or to joy coming from different sources but to the fullness of the joy. The cause of his joy, or rejoicing, was their faith, their steadfastness in their affliction, but God was the One who had sustained the saints in the midst of persecution. Thus in giving thanks to God for this rejoicing he was giving thanks to God for sustaining the saints at Thessalonica.

"before our God; Indicating an inward rejoicing before God rather than what is outward and before men. This joy was not the transient joviality of the world, but a rejoicing over the spiritual well being of saints and which had the approval of God.

Verse 10. **"Night and day praying exceedingly"** This is another effect of the news that Timothy brought. Firstly encouragement, then rejoicing and thanksgiving, and now constant prayer. The word 'exceedingly' indicates the intensity and the fervency of his prayer and it shows that his prayer was constant. What about our prayer life? Is it marked by fervency, intensity and constancy?

"that we might see your face," Paul now gives the content of his prayer. It was that he might see them again, as he had sought to do (2:18). Not just for his own sake, but also for their personal benefit. His actual presence would be beneficial to them (see Rom 1:10-11). He had their spiritual well being at heart.

"and might perfect". The Greek word translated 'perfect' is translated 'mending', in Matt 4:21, 'restore' in Gal 6:1, 'prepared' in Heb 10:5 and 'framed' in Heb 11:1. It has the meaning of to order, to confirm, to complete or to render fit. Here the idea is of fully equipping their faith or completing their faith.

"that which is lacking" Although the apostle had commended their faith there was still something lacking or wanting as to **the faith**. The idea is of that which is deficient and refers to that which Paul had been unable to impart to them because of his sudden departure from Thessalonica. Doctrine is so vital to the child of God and it is the fertile ground in which the tree of true Christian character flourishes. We must build upon the solid foundation of the Word of God - all other ground is sinking sand.

"in your faith?" This refers to the body of truth which had been committed to them. His affection was so great for them that he longed to return. He knew that there was a need for further instruction, for further truth to be imparted to them. This would demand a further response resulting in further spiritual progress. There is always a demand upon believers to respond to the truth of God and there is always a need for spiritual progress. The only basis of spiritual development, holiness of life and Christlikeness is the truth of God.

Verse 11. **"NOW"** Here he gives expression to his desire and prayer.

"God himself" The apostle invokes the august majesty and power of the Almighty God, knowing that he alone is the direct Controller of events. How essential it is for us to appreciate the greatness, sovereignty and holiness of God.

"and our Father," Paul appreciates the relationship with God into which divine grace has brought the saints. The Almighty God is now our Father.

"and our Lord Jesus Christ," The One to whom all saints belong and to whom they are responsible as servants. No doubt the deity of Christ is also indicated here - co-equal and co-eternal with the Father yet personally distinct from the Father.

"direct our way unto you." The idea is to make direct or straighten our way - it refers to the removing of the obstacles used by Satan to prevent Paul from coming to Thessalonica. The verb 'direct' is singular, thus the Father and the Son are linked as one in ordering the steps of the servants of God. In this way the absolute unity of the Father and the Son is expressed. If God opened the way Satan would not be able to prevent the servants visiting Thessalonica.

Verse 12. The continuation of Paul's desire and prayer, but now on the behalf of the Thessalonian believers.

"And the Lord" It is stated that this could refer to either the Father or the Son. However, throughout these epistles this title generally refers to the Lord Jesus Christ.

"make you to increase and abound in love" Love can only be known by its actions and always expends itself for the benefit of others. He has already mentioned that he had received good tidings of their love, but he now expresses his desire that it might grow and overflow - an enlargement and an overflowing in that love which they were already manifesting. Whereas God alone is the object of the Christian's faith, men as well as God should be the object of the believer's love. God must be the primary object of our love which will be practically manifested or expressed in love to our fellow believers and to all.

"one toward another," First of all their love towards each other must grow, for this is indeed a commandment of the Lord - "A new commandment I give unto you, That ye love one another" (John 13:34; 15:12). They were under the severe pressure of persecution and love towards each other was so vital in such circumstances.

"and toward all men," Their love was not only to be enlarged and abound towards each other but towards all men. It is the duty of believers to manifest love to all (Matt 5:43-48; Rom 13:10; James 2:8). Christian love, whether towards fellow believers or to unbelievers is not a mere emotion but shows itself in seeking their welfare. Self-will, self-pleasure, self-centeredness are all features that are opposite to Christian love.

"even as we do toward you:" The servants were an example of Christian love - the spending of themselves on the behalf of the Thessalonians. The expression also implies the constancy of Paul's love for them and shows them that he was exhorting them to do what he practised himself. Of course the perfect example of this is our blessed Lord. The exercise of love to others builds up our own Christian character. Love is the basis of what follows in verse 13 - the establishing of the heart.

Verse 13. **"To the end he may stablish"** Love is not an end in itself but a means to some end, and here it is holiness that is in view. Stablish means to establish or to strengthen. The tense emphasises purpose - the end in view being to establish their hearts.

"your hearts unblameable in holiness" Unblameable is to be free from every valid charge. Here it is being unblameable in the sphere of holiness. The believer is sanctified as to position or standing before God, but he must seek to live in keeping with that fact now. Holiness in life is what God expects of every child of God - "as he which hath called you is holy, so be ye holy in all manner of conversation; Because it is written, Be ye holy; for I am holy." (1 Peter 1:15-16). Where there is holiness and love there is no blame. One has stated, "they must so live now that they will stand unblameable in holiness before God as Judge, the searcher of the hearts of men" (Wiles). It is suggested that the apostle is now linking the present with the future and W.E.Vine paraphrases thus, "The Lord enable you more and more to spend your lives in the interests of others, in order that He may establish you in Christian character now, that you may be vindicated from every charge that may be brought against you at the Judgement Seat of Christ." Most certainly we must live now in the light of the Judgement Seat of Christ. There should be progress in a life of holiness now but the perfection in holiness will be attained only when the Lord comes.

"before God, even our Father," In front of God, even our Father. It is true that we should be characterised by love and holiness before God now but this expression has reference to a future day and not to the omnipresence of God. The idea is that of being before or presented before God, even our Father. It is further explained by the next expression.

"at the coming of our Lord Jesus Christ" The Greek word 'parousia' is again used as in chapter 2:19 and carries the idea of presence - at the presence of our Lord Jesus Christ with all His saints. It is not the coming of the Lord to earth that is in view but that day when all the saints, in the presence of the Lord Jesus Christ, will be before God, even our Father. Although many link this verse with the Judgement Seat of Christ we suggest that the introduction into the Father's House is in view.

"with all his saints." 'With' indicates association and companionship - here it has the idea of among, amidst or in company with. We feel it speaks of that day when the Lord Jesus Christ, in company with all His saints, will be before the Father - "Behold I and the children which God hath given me" (Heb 2:13). It is not only Christ before the Father but Christ along with all His saints. This is the triumph of the gospel and the transformation of the saints. 'All' - no such thing as a partial rapture. All the saints are there.

An appreciation of the imminent return of the Lord along with the anticipation of the father's House will cause us to be steadfast in a life of love and holiness now.

CHAPTER 4

Doctrinal

In this chapter the Christian life is brought before us in relation to God (verses 1-2), in relation to ourselves (verses 3-8), in relation to our fellow believers (verses 9-10), in relation to the world without (verses 11-12) and in relation to the saints that sleep (verses 13-18). The chapter is divided into two main sections:- Verses 1-12 Exhortation as to their conduct and Verses 13-18 Instruction in order to alleviate their concern. It has been suggested that in Verses 1-12 we have doctrine in relation to conduct and in Verses 13-18 we have doctrine in relation to comfort. In the first twelve verses the apostle writes about things which they know but in the rest of the chapter he writes about things which they do not know.

Verses 1-12 Exhortation

This section develops out of the closing verses of chapter 3 where we have both holiness and love mentioned. The section can be divided into three parts:- 1. Verses 1-8 The purity of life - an appeal for personal chastity, 2. Verses 9-10 The progress of love - an appeal for personal charity (love) and 3. Verses 11-12 The power of testimony - an appeal for personal control.

Verses 1-8 The Purity Expected

This passage is a little difficult and somewhat delicate. The first two verses are general in character but lead to the specific subject of sanctification in verses 3-8. The apostle reminds them of their responsibility towards what they had already been taught and appeals to them to conduct themselves accordingly.

Verse 1. The two verbs 'beseech' and 'exhort' emphasise the importance of the subject with which the apostle is dealing.

"Furthermore" Although the Greek word is translated 'finally' in Phil 3:1 and 2 Thess 3:1 it has the idea of 'remaining' or 'as to the rest'. The apostle is not bringing the epistle to a close but introducing practical exhortations. The word could also indicate that the apostle is now seeking to supply any deficiency that may have resulted from his sudden departure from Thessalonica (see Chapter 3:10).

"then" Translated 'therefore' in Chapter 5:6 - this indicates the link between the close of chapter 3 and the exhortation Paul is about to make. As he has mentioned his prayer in relation to their holiness in Chapter 3:13, so now he is going to exhort them to that end.

"we beseech you, brethren," To ask or request. The tense suggests urgency and the word places the emphasis upon the Thessalonians to act upon what they have already learned.

"and exhort you by the Lord Jesus," The word translated 'exhort' occurs eight times in this epistle and three times in this chapter. It is translated 'beseech' in verse 10 and 'comfort' in verse 18. It has the thought here of exhortation, entreaty or appealing. Again the tense suggests urgency. The expression 'by or in the Lord Jesus' is only linked with the verb exhort. Paul beseeches or requests on his own account because of his relationship with them and because of his love for them. However, he exhorts them because of their relationship to the Lord and because of the sphere in which they should live. The Lordship of Christ makes demands upon the child of God.

"that as ye have received of us" The apostle is referring to the teaching he and his companions had given at Thessalonica and their reception of that teaching, which should have affected their personal lives. The truth of God should always have a practical impact upon the lives of believers. This is clear from the next expression:-

"how ye ought to walk" Walk, as in Chapter 2:12, has reference to the manner of life - the activities and moral conduct of each individual. The Greek word translated 'ought' indicates necessity and is translated 'must' in many passages (e.g. 1 Tim 3:2, 7). The believer's manner of life must be in keeping with the teaching of the Word of God. This is not a choice but an obligation to be carried out. Our manner of life should be in keeping with the gospel we heard and believed, demonstrating the effect of that message upon ours lives (Phil 1:27). We should walk in newness of life, displaying the kind of life that is ours because of union with our risen and glorified Lord and Saviour (Rom 6:4). Our behaviour should be in keeping with being the children of light, not as others in the vanity of their minds (Eph 4:17; 5:8), conducting ourselves in keeping with the truth and after the commandments of the Lord (2 John 4, 6).

"and to please God," The word 'please' has the thought of bringing pleasure to, or being acceptable to God. The tense indicates a continual or habitual activity which is pleasurable to God. In Chapter 2:4 it is used in relation to service and in Chapter 2:15 it is used negatively of the Jews. Here it is used in relation to the believer's walk of life. Enoch walked with God (Gen 5:24) and thus had this testimony, that he pleased God (Heb 11:5). Enoch enjoyed the divine Presence and thus sought to please God in all things. This should be the characteristic of every child of God. A delight in the Lord's presence will produce diligence in seeking to please Him.

"so ye would abound more and more." Paul was never content with past achievements as he knew that there was always room for improvement. The appeal is that there be an increasing conformity to the truth that they had received, in order to bring greater pleasure to God - an abundance of spiritual development. Is there an abundance of spiritual growth in our lives? Are we pressing towards a greater conformity to the truth of God in our daily lives? Here Paul writes of abounding more and more in one's life whereas in verse 10 he writes of increasing more and more in love.

Verse 2. **"For ye know what commandments we gave you"**

What Paul and his fellow labourers had taught them were indeed commandments in relation to their walk - their manner of life. The word translated 'commandments' carries the idea of orders received from a superior to be passed on to others. Here it refers to the special teaching or precepts on Christian behaviour which had been given by the servants when in Thessalonica.

"by the Lord Jesus." Although Paul had apostolic authority this was only derived from the Lord and thus the commandments given to the Thessalonians were really from the Lord. Not to act according to those commandments would be disobedience to the Lord Himself. Here the apostle is referring to the verbal teaching they received at Thessalonica whereas in 1 Cor 14:37 he applies the same principle to his written ministry to the Corinthians.

Verse 3. Having made his appeal regarding their walk and spiritual development, Paul now comes to the specific subject of sanctification, particularly in relation to morality. There are two suggestions as to the teaching of verses 3-8:- 1) that there are two subjects dealt with - sexual uncleanness and dishonesty in business and 2) that only sexual uncleanness is in view. We believe that the second is more in keeping with the passage. The subject is an important one and so necessary in the day in which we live. The passage is difficult and delicate yet the teaching emphasises the purity of life that is demanded of the child of God.

"For this is the will of God," There is no definite article before 'will' indicating that what the apostle is going to deal with is but part of the will of God, yet an important part that has a practical affect upon our lives. The thought here is not of the determined purpose of God but of the design and desire of God in relation to the practical moral life of the child of God. What Paul has called the commandments in the previous verse he now calls the will of God.

"even your sanctification," There are two aspects of sanctification; the second proceeding from the first. The first is absolute or positional which God has provided for every believer - He has set us apart to Himself and for His glory. The second is practical and has to do with the life of those who have been set apart to God. The positive side is that believers have been set apart **to** and **for** God and should live in keeping with what God has done. The negative side is that believers have been set apart by God **from** all that is contrary to Him and should live accordingly. Here it has reference to purity or chastity in contrast to immorality as indicated in the next expression.

"that ye should abstain from fornication:" We must appreciate that these Thessalonian believers had been steeped in idolatry and that idolatry and immorality are joined together. Linked with heathen temples were priestesses who were set apart to prostitution and linked with the temple worship was every kind of uncleanness. Today, every kind of immorality is prevalent in society. The word 'abstain' carries the thought of holding one's self back from some action or keeping one's self from uncleanness. Here we have the negative side of sanctification. Although the English dictionary gives the meaning of 'fornication' as sexual intercourse of unmarried persons or of an unmarried with a married person the Greek word translated 'fornication' in its general sense, we are told, embraces every kind of sexual uncleanness. Many believe that the word is used in this general way here whereas others believe it is used in a restricted way linking verses 3-5 with premarital promiscuity and verse 6 with adultery. We know that there are those who state that 'fornication' is never used in a restricted way in the Scriptures. Some say that the word fornication always embraces adultery. However, we cannot agree with that statement since it would imply that in such passages as Matt 15:19, Mark 7:21 22; Gal 5:19-21 the word adultery would be superfluous since it would be included in the word fornication. The same would apply to the associated words whoremongers (fornicators) and adulterers in Heb 13:4. We do not believe that the Lord or the Spirit of God used any word that was unnecessary. Without making any further comment on the above we believe that the child of God should abstain from every kind of sexual uncleanness. In this day of gross uncleanness the believer should stand out as being pure in mind and holy in life. We as believers should encourage the younger members of our families to view other believers of their age as brothers and sisters in Christ and not as potential marriage partners. We should encourage young believers to pray earnestly about marriage partners and strongly discourage the worldly practice of flirtation. In this permissive society believers should be aware of the dangers and not place themselves in a situation where they are exposed to temptation. We should appreciate the seriousness of marriage and the solemnity of the marriage vows avoiding immorality before and after marriage. The world has cast away all morals, treating marriage lightly, making divorce and re-marriage common practice and applauding co-habitation, but God's standard remains unchanged and cannot be lowered. It behoves older believers to set a good example.

Verse 4. **"That every one of you"** No one is excluded from this solemn exhortation. Every believer is expected to take heed of the teaching of the Word of God and expected to allow that teaching to mould his (or her) life. The particular teaching here is moral purity and every believer needs to be on guard - "let him that thinketh he standeth take heed lest he fall." (1 Cor 10:12).

"should know how to possess his vessel" 'Know how' is the knowledge or skill necessary to accomplish a particular purpose. It has been suggested that in the context this has the idea of respect. The word translated 'possess' has the idea of obtaining, acquiring or procuring for one's self and thus to possess. It is translated 'purchased' in Acts 1:18; 8:20 and 'obtained' in Acts 22:28. There are two main schools of thought in regard to the expression 'his vessel' - 1) that the word vessel is a metaphor for the body (2 Cor 4:7) and thus would be linked with 1 Cor 9:27, and 2) that it is a metaphor for wife (1 Peter 3:7 and by implication husband) and thus would be linked with 1 Cor 7:2. In view of the verb 'possess' the second seems more in keeping with the context and thus the thought that protection from fornication consists in carrying on the divinely instituted plan of marriage - one man and one woman for life. Although we favour this second view either would emphasise the importance of sexual purity which is so obviously the message here.

"in sanctification and honour:" In sanctification could either be the purpose of possessing his own vessel or the idea of being set apart to and for one's self - i.e the wife set apart exclusively for the husband and by implication the husband set apart exclusively for the wife. The word translated 'honour' has to do with value and esteem, and is translated 'price' in 1 Cor 6:20 and 'precious' in 1 Peter 2:7. W.E. Vine states, "the view that the 'vessel' signifies the wife, and that the reference is to the sanctified maintenance of the married state, is supported by the facts that in 1 Pet 3:7 the same word honour is used with regard to the wife. Again in Heb 13:4 honourable is used in regard to marriage". Should the word 'vessel' signify 'the body' then the word honour would carry the thought of value as belonging to God and thus it should be used accordingly.

Verse 5. **"Not in the lust of concupiscence,"** The idea in the word translated 'lust' is that of passion. It is found only in two other passages where it is translated 'affections' in Rom 1:26 (vile passion) and 'inordinate affection' in Col 3:5 (depraved passion). The word translated 'concupiscence' is translated 'desire' in chapter 2:17 but mainly translated 'lust' (see Rom 1:24; Gal 5:16). The word carries the thought of longing or yearning and is sometimes used in a good sense as in chapter 2:17; Luke 22:15 and Phil 1:23. However, it is generally used in a bad sense as it is here. It has been said that the first word is the evil state from which the second word springs - thus the passion of lust (either of the flesh or the mind - Eph 2:3). Here it seems to be in relation to the flesh since unchastity is the subject. Trench describes 'passion' as the diseased condition out of which 'lust' springs.

"even as" Just as (see Chapter 3:6) - the apostle now gives an example of such lustful passion.

"the Gentiles which know not God:" The Thessalonians were themselves Gentiles but they had responded to the gospel message and had turned to God from idols. Their lives had been completely changed. However, they were fully aware of the idolatrous and immoral behaviour of the Gentiles in general who had deliberately turned away from God, not desiring to retain God in their knowledge (Rom 1:28). The whole section in Rom 1:18-32 unfolds the gross immorality of the Gentiles who know not God. Within that section we note sexual uncleanness, sordid things, condemned by God, yet legalised by Governments and practised today (see Rom 1:26-27). Only the emancipating power of the gospel can deliver men from such dreadful behaviour. Thus Paul shows that sanctification is being set apart from the unclean practices of those who do not know God. Believers are expected to conduct themselves differently to those who are not saved.

Verse 6. **"That no man go beyond"** The word translated 'beyond' is only found here and means to transgress, to trespass, to step over or to overstep the proper limit. The idea here seems to be stepping over the line that divides chastity and uncleanness, of trespassing in relation to what belongs to another.

"and defraud his brother in any matter:" The word translated 'defraud' is only found elsewhere in 2 Corinthians - Chapter 2:11 (get an advantage); Chapter 7:2 (defrauded); and Chapter 12:17, 18 (make a gain). It means to gain from another or to take advantage of another. It also has the idea of covetousness or to selfishly make gain for one's own gratification by disregarding another's right. 'His brother' - W.E. Vine writes, "though there is no other instance in Paul's Epp. Of the use of this word of mankind in general, it is difficult to suppose that the apostle here limited its meaning to the Christian relationship; cp. Matt 7:3." There is a definite article before the word 'matter' indicating the apostle is continuing the subject of the previous verses - chastity. Here it is the forbidding of transgressing the bounds of marriage where a man takes another man's wife, thus defrauding him - forbidding stepping over the line by usurping the use of another man's wife. How sad that this takes place among those who claim to belong to Christ.

"because" For this reason or these reasons - on this account.

"that the Lord is the avenger of all such," The first reason for chastity - for not crossing the line between chastity and uncleanness. The word translated 'avenger' means one who meets out justice or exacts a penalty and is only found elsewhere in Rom 13:4 (revenger). "Vengeance is mine; I will repay, saith the Lord" (Rom 12:19; Deut 32:35). God will deal righteously with all who violates His law of chastity - "Marriage is honourable in all, and the bed undefiled: but whoremongers and adulterers God will judge." (Heb 13:4). All who violate the sanctity of marriage will reap the consequences. We know that where there is true repentance there is forgiveness but there can be sad consequences from such sin. The principle of Gal 6:7 applies to believers as well as unbelievers - "whatsoever a man soweth, that shall he also reap."

"as we also have forewarned you and testified." While at Thessalonica the servants, through their teaching, had informed the saints of the justice and righteousness of God and of the importance of purity in their lives. This would have included the consequences of violating chastity. The word translated 'testified' means to declare or charge solemnly (1 Tim 5:21), to solemnly affirm or to bear full and complete witness. The idea here is that Paul and his companions thoroughly or constantly testified of these things when they were with them. The apostle is reminding them of the teaching relative to purity of life. We need to remind our hearts of the clear teaching in the Scriptures of Christian purity and fidelity. In this wicked world we need to remember constantly the charge to be pure.

Verse 7. **"For God hath not called us unto uncleanness,"** This verse brings before us the second reason for chastity and looks back to what God has done. The word translated 'called' means to call with an object in view (Rom 8:30; 1 Cor 1:9; Gal 5:13).

The tense indicates a definite action in the past which refers to the call of the gospel to which the Thessalonians had responded. First of all the call of God is expressed negatively - not unto uncleanness. The preposition translated 'unto' carries the idea of 'with a view to' and with the negative forbids uncleanness. The word translated 'uncleanness' (as Chapter 2:3) indicates here moral impurity. When they were in their idolatrous state, the Thessalonians lived in the lust of uncleanness but God, through the gospel, had called them, not to continue in their immoral state, but to a life of purity. The gospel itself is indeed a condemnation of impurity and is yet a message of deliverance from all uncleanness.

"but unto holiness." The preposition translated 'unto' here is different to the previous one and has the thought of 'in the element or sphere of' indicating the sphere of the Christian life is holiness. W.E. Vine states, "The thought is apparently that the Christian is to live his life in a holy atmosphere". Separation from the world is important to avoid defilement and contamination - "to keep himself unspotted from the world" (James 1:27) - "For all that is in the world, the lust of the flesh, and the lust of the eyes, and the pride of life, is not of the Father, but is of the world" (1 John 2:16). The word translated 'holiness' is translated ' sanctification' in verses 3 - 4 and refers to the conduct befitting those sanctified by God - the condition of holiness resulting from the call of God. "As he which hath called you is holy, so be ye holy in all manner of conversation; Because it is written, Be ye holy; for I am holy." (1 Peter 1:15-16). The call of God, through the gospel, enables the believer to live in purity.

Verse 8. **"He therefore that despiseth,"** The word 'therefore' emphasises the conclusion that follows. The word translated 'despiseth' is used of rejecting Christ (John 12:48); of bringing to nothing the understanding of the prudent (1 Cor 1:19); of frustrating the grace of God (Gal 2:21 - which Paul did not do); of disannulling (Gal 3:15); and of casting off faith (1 Tim 5:12). The thought here is of rejecting or disregarding the teaching of the apostle mentioned in previous verses. How sad when believers set aside or disregard the teaching of the holy scriptures which should govern their lives.

"despiseth not man, but God," In despising the teaching on chastity it was not men (those who had taught them) they despised, but God (see Luke 10:16). To despise the truth of God is to despise God Himself. This teaching contains the unchanging laws of God and to set aside those laws is to reject God Himself. Thus Paul emphasises the seriousness of ignoring or making void this teaching on moral purity. How important it is, in a day of laxity, to appreciate the seriousness of immorality.

"who hath also given unto us his holy Spirit." This statement not only further emphasises the seriousness of moral uncleanness but also indicates to us the power which enables us to live in purity. The emphasis here is on the word 'holy' in keeping with the subject of holiness. Since the gracious Holy Spirit indwells every child of God, for any believer to ignore the teaching on holiness would be to do despite to the Holy Spirit. The Holy Spirit has taken up permanent residence in the body of the believer in order to take practical possession of that body and to use it exclusively for the pleasure and glory of God, to whom it belongs (1 Cor 6:18-20). Thus the infinite power of the Holy Spirit is available to us, enabling us to overcome temptation and to live holy lives.

2. Verses 9-10 The Progress Desired
We now pass from the subject of sanctification to the subject of brotherly love.

Verse 9. **"BUT"** A transitional word indicating a contrast to the previous section - a contrast between the new subject of brotherly love and the sin of uncleanness.

"as touching brotherly love" The Greek word translated brotherly love is 'philadelphia' and comes from two Greek words 'phileo' or 'philia' (love, affection) and 'adelphos' (brother, from the same womb), i.e. brother love. Apart from Rev 3 it is only found six times in the New Testament (Rom 12:10; Heb 13:1; 1 Pet 1:22; 2 Pet 1:7 and here). In Rom 12:10 philadelphia is linked with the tender affection of family relationship, indicating that all believers, being in the same family, have the responsibility of loving one another - "Whosoever believeth that Jesus is the Christ is born of God: and every one that loveth him that begat loveth him also that is begotten of him" (1 John 5:1). In Heb 13:1 the stress is on the continuance of brotherly love in contrast to the things which shall be removed in chapter 12. It is important that we cultivate brotherly love, not allowing anything to hinder its flow to fellow believers, for it is a command of the Lord Himself as well as a manifestation of discipleship (John 13:34-35). In 1 Pet 1:22 philadelphia (love of the brethren) is linked with the new birth and should be exercised in sincerity (unfeigned), purity (out of a pure heart) and fervently - "That ye love one another, as I have loved you." (John 15:12). In 2 Pet 1:7 the word is translated 'brotherly kindness' and is used twice in the progress of spiritual development and character expected of every believer. This love is not a mere sentiment but manifests itself in seeking the well being of each other and in deeds of kindness (see 1 John 3:16-18).

"ye need not that I write unto you:" Again a contrast to the previous subject about which it was needful to write. Besides his own knowledge Paul gives the reason in the next expression.

"for ye yourselves are taught of God to love one another." The Greek word translated 'taught of God' only occurs here. Although the servants would have taught the Thessalonian believers to love one another this expression indicates that God Himself has implanted the knowledge of mutual love in the hearts of the saints. This takes place the moment a person is born into the family of God – "We know that we have passed from death unto life, because we love the brethren" (1 John 3:14 – see also 1 John 2:27). The Greek word translated love is 'agape' which is used of the love of God and indicates a selfless, sacrificing love. Love should permeate our thoughts, control our speech and govern our actions. We are to love our fellow believers even as God loves us. We notice that in verse 3 we have the will of God, in verse 7 we have the call of God, in verse 8 we have the gift of God and here we have being taught of God.

Verse 10. **"And indeed ye do it"** The apostle had seen a manifestation of their love while he was with them and now acknowledges this fact. They had not only been taught but had put into practice that teaching. It is vital that we put into practice the teaching of the Word of God.

"toward all the brethren which are in all Macedonia:" Their love reached out beyond their own circle in Thessalonica embracing believers in the province of Macedonia, when the opportunity arose, where there were a number of assemblies. Our love to fellow believers should never be partial or restricted but should be towards all believers as opportunity arises. **"we beseech you, brethren,"** For 'beseech' see 'exhort' in verse 1. We again see the tenderness of the Apostle in this exhortation by his use of the word brethren.

"that ye increase more and more;" As with every Christian feature there is always room for improvement. There ought to be an increasing development of the features seen in perfection in our blessed Lord and Saviour. The feature here is love not one's walk, as mentioned in verse 1, and we should abound more and more in love, ever seeking to reach the standard of perfection seen in Christ.

3. Verses 11-12 The Power of Testimony
The contrast commenced in verse 9 continues but now it is between the sin of uncleanness and honesty of life. As some have suggested, a life of testimony springs from practical sanctification.

Verse 11. **"And that ye study to be quiet,"** The Greek word translated 'study' only occurs elsewhere in Rom 15: 20 (strived) and 2 Cor 5:9 (labour) and literally means to be fond of honour. It carries the thought of striving to a certain end. Both love and honour are included in the word, thus the idea of exerting one's self out of love and a sense of honour – let it be your ambition or make it your aim. The Greek word translated 'quiet' is found five times in the New Testament, being translated 'held their peace' (Luke 14:4; Acts 11:18), 'rested' (Luke 23:56) and 'ceased' (Acts 21:14), and carries the idea of silence or of being at rest. We are to be ambitious or diligent to live a quiet or tranquil life in the midst of the rush and bustle of the world.

"and to do your own business," The idea here is to see to one's own affairs or things. Linking it with the previous expression the exhortation would be to lead a quiet life actively engaged in one's own affairs without interfering or meddling in the affairs of others. However, that does not mean we must only look after our selves for we are exhorted to seek the welfare of others (1 Cor 10:24: Phil 2:4).

"and to work with your own hands," To be industrious in providing for one's own material needs and to help others in need (see Eph 4:28). It is evident from 2 Thess 3:11 that there were among the Thessalonians those who did not work but were content to take advantage of the kindness of their fellow believers. This then is not only a condemnation of idleness, which should never characterise the child of God, but also a commandment to be carried out.

"as we commanded you;" This refers to the commands give when Paul and his companions were in Thessalonica. Idleness and prying into the affairs of others mars the Christian Testimony and dishonours the Lord to whom we profess to belong. It also undermines the message of the gospel we profess to believe and we proclaim.

Verse 12. **"That ye may walk honestly"** The word translated 'honestly' only occurs elsewhere in Rom 13:13 and 1 Cor 14:40 (decently) and has the idea of orderly or becomingly. The deportment of the child of God should not only be in keeping with the message of the gospel but should enhance that message which idleness would mar.

"toward them that are without," The believer's manner of life should be marked by diligence and orderliness as a witness to unbelievers. The effect of the gospel is to be seen in the daily life of the child of God even in the midst of opposition. In order to live in keeping with the character and claims of God the believer must live a separated life, a life that is different to the world and which will often result in hostility from unbelievers. However, the believer will have a clear conscience before God and no valid charge could be made against such a manner of life (see 1 Peter 2:15; 3:16). Is our manner of life bearing an affective testimony and is it bringing pleasure and glory to God?

"and that ye may have lack of nothing." That by their own labours they may provide for their needs and not be a burden to others which would become a stumbling block to unbelievers.

The apostle mentions three things in verse 11:-

(i) Do not have a restless spirit but make it your aim be live quietly.
(ii) Do not be a busybody but see to your own affairs.
(iii) Do not be lazy or idle but work.

He then gives two reasons in verse 12:-

(i) That your manner of life might be honest – your testimony before men is important so do not mar it.
(ii) That you lack nothing – you have no need to depend upon others for the necessary things of life.

Verses 13-18 Instruction
It is clear from Chapter 1:9-10 that the Thessalonian believers were not ignorant regarding the fact of the coming again of the Lord Jesus Christ. However, it seems that they had confined the coming to the living saints and had expected the Lord to come within the limits of their life time. Paul had not taught them that the Lord would come in their life time but the truth of the Lord's coming had been taught them in such a way that it was the immediate hope of their hearts. However, some of their number had died, causing them deep anxiety. As yet no revelation from

God had been given concerning the dead in Christ. They were not ignorant of the truth of resurrection but they were ignorant regarding the time of the resurrection of their fellow believers who had died. This passage deals with that anxiety and was intended to bring comfort to their hearts. We can divide the passage into four parts:- 1. V13 The Problem Stated; 2. V14 The Problem Solved; 3. V14-17 The Particulars Unfolded; V18 The Result of the Revelation.

Verse 13 The Problem Stated
"BUT I would not have you to be ignorant, brethren," This expression starts a new subject of which the Thessalonian had no knowledge which is in contrast to their understanding of brotherly love in the previous verses. This subject contains a direct revelation from the Lord which was intended to moderate their sorrow concerning the death of some of their fellow believers (see next expression). The Greek word translated 'ignorant' means lack of knowledge or understanding. It seems that their ignorance concerning those who had died was causing them perplexity, great or excessive sorrow and anxiety. They had been taught, by Paul and his companions, about the Kingship of the Lord Jesus Christ and concerning His coming kingdom and that they would share in the glory of that kingdom. This is proved by the charge in Acts 17:7 and the statement of 1 Thess 2:12. Now some of their fellow believers had died and this caused them great anxiety. Would those believers who had died miss the glory of the kingdom? This was a vexing problem which was bringing them deep sorrow and distress. The words of the Lord Jesus recorded in John 11:25-26 and John 14:1-3 had not yet been written and so could afford them no comfort. Thus they were greatly troubled and grieved for those who had died.

"concerning them which are asleep," The Greek word translated 'asleep' comes from a word meaning 'to lie down'. Here it is used metaphorically of the death of believers (see Acts 7:60; 1 Cor 15:6, 18, 20). The tense here indicates what is on going - those who have fallen asleep and who are falling asleep. The English word cemetery comes from a related word which means 'the sleeping place'. We must point out that this word refers only to the physical body of the believer and not to the soul. There is no such thing as soul sleep in the Word of God. The metaphor here is apt, as sleep is only temporary and has its awaking just as when the believer's body is raised. When a believer falls asleep that believer is absent from the body but present with the Lord (2 Cor 5:8) which is very far better (Phil 1:23).

"that ye sorrow not," The apostle is not condemning believers who express grief at the loss of fellow believers. This is a normal experience for all. However there should be a difference between their grief and the grief of unbelievers, as this verse shows.

"even as others which have no hope." The expression 'even as others (the rest - in contrast to them as believers)' contrasts the sorrow of believers with the sorrow of unbelievers. The grief of believers is different to the grief of unbelievers for the unbeliever has no hope (Eph 2:12) whereas the believer has a lively (living) and blessed hope (1 Pet 1:3; Titus 2:13). Thus there is joy as well as sorrow at the Home call of fellow believers - joy because they are absent from the body and present with the Lord, sorrow because their presence and help will be missed.

Verse 14 The Problem Solved
"For if we believe that Jesus died" Here we have something of significance - a deliberate contrast between the term 'sleep' in relation to believers and the word 'died' used here of the Lord Jesus. When a believer dies this passage tells us he falls asleep. Death has no terror for the believer since it has been robbed of its sting. The believer will not know death in all its dreadfulness. This is borne out in relation to Stephen who died a cruel and painful death and yet we read "he fell asleep" (Acts 7:60). But that word 'sleep' is never used concerning the Lord Jesus because He entered into death. He knew death in all its dreadfulness, in all its exceeding bitterness. The sting of death had not been drawn out for Him as He bore our sins on the cross. Only because of our sins did He enter into that horror of

great darkness - "for the sufferings of death . . . taste death for every man" (Heb 2:9).

"and rose again," The death and resurrection of Christ are fundamental truths of the gospel (see 1 Cor 15:3-4) - "Who was delivered for our offences, and was raised again for our justification" (Rom 4:25). To deny the physical resurrection of Christ is to undermine the foundation of the gospel.

"even so them also which sleep in Jesus" "Even so . . . also" is the link between the two fundamental facts of the gospel and what follows. W.E. Vine states the phrase runs, "if we believe, as we do, that Jesus died and rose again, even so we believe also -." The resurrection of the Lord Jesus Christ is the assurance of the resurrection of the believer (1 Cor 15:20-23). "Which sleep in or through Jesus" - the believer is put to sleep by Jesus - this is a delightful expression.

"will God bring with him." There are at least three suggestions regarding this expression:-

(i) Just as God raised up Jesus from among the dead so, in association with Him, will God raise from the dead those believers who have been put to sleep.

(ii) That at the Rapture God will bring with the Lord Jesus the spirits of those who have been put to sleep and reunite them with their bodies.

(iii) That God will bring the redeemed of this day of grace with the Lord Jesus at His glorious manifestation.

We suggest the third is more in keeping with the passage. We know from Heb 1:6 that God will again bring the Lord Jesus into the world. Then He will come in His glory as the Mighty Potentate to hold to account all who have filled the earth with lawlessness and rebellion against God (Rev 19:19-21). He will come in all His Majesty as the King of kings and Lord of lords to sit upon the throne of His glory (Rev 19:16; Matt 25:31). In that day of His manifestation, when He establishes His glorious kingdom,

God will bring with him the saints of this day of grace to share His glory (Col 3:4). In that day Christ will be glorified in His saints and will be admired in all them that believe (2 Thess 1:10). However, the question would arise, "How can this be since most of the Thessalonian believers were on earth and some of their number had died?" In the following verses the apostle answers this dilemma by revealing that, before the manifestation of Christ, another event is going to take place. Those who were asleep would be resurrected when the Lord comes as the Great Conqueror of death to take His own to be forever with Him.

Verses 15-17 The Particulars Unfolded
Verse 15. **"For this we say unto you by the word of the Lord,"** The idea here is that of a word Paul had received from the risen Lord, which carried the authenticity of the Lord. In this, the first of Paul's inspired epistles, the apostle unfolds that special word from the risen Lord which was given in order to banish the ignorance of the Thessalonians concerning their fellow believers. This revelation would solve their problem, comfort their hearts and enlighten their understanding. The answer to their problem was that the Lord will come again as the Great Conqueror of death, before He comes to establish His glorious kingdom.

"that we which are alive" We that are alive in contrast to those believers who had died. Here the apostle associates himself with the living believers because, at the time of writing this epistle, the Lord's coming was His expectation as well as their expectation.

"and remain" The Greek word translated 'remain' is only found here and verse 17 and has the thought of being left - those who are left. Some suggest that the idea is of those who are left to the coming of Christ. Others suggest it is in contrast to those who have been taken and are absent from the body and present with the Lord (2 Cor 5:8).

"unto the coming of the Lord" Once again we have the Greek word 'parousia' but here it is used of that moment when the

Lord will come to take away His redeemed from this world. We have said that the word not only refers to the moment of the Lord's arrival to take away His own, but also embraces the events which will take place in heaven subsequent to the rapture and prior to the Lord's manifestation.

"shall not prevent them that are asleep." The Greek word translated 'prevent' means to precede and has the thought here of going before. The apostle is assuring the Thessalonian believers that the death of believers does not place them at any disadvantage when the Lord comes.

Verse 16. **"For the Lord himself shall descend from heaven"** Paul now begins to give the details that substantiate the previous statements he has made. 'The Lord Himself' - the One Who died and rose triumphant from among the dead (Verse 14). The One Who ascended far above all and Who sat down on the right hand of the Majesty on high (Heb 1:3). He now comes down to call away His own out of this world. This is the fulfilment of His promise to His disciples - "I will come again and receive you unto myself" (John 14:3). It has been suggested that this expression is in contrast to the expression in verse 14 'will God bring with him'.

"with" Three things accompany the Lord's descent. A number of explanations as to the significance of these three things have been made. We can only offer suggestions for personal consideration.

"a shout," We take it that the shout comes from the Lord Himself as in John 5:25 and 11:43. The word only occurs here and means a summons or a shout of command. Some suggest it refers to the Lord's command to all the saints of this day of grace while others suggest that it is a command only to the dead in Christ.

"the voice of the archangel," Because there are no definite articles this statement could speak of the quality of the shout - as a voice like an archangel. However some suggest that this has reference to Michael (Jude 9) who, as leader of angelic forces, will be present to escort the saints through enemy territory.

"And with the trump of God:" The trump here could be linked with the last trump of 1 Cor 15:52 but cannot be linked with the last of the seven trumpets in Rev 11:15. The trump here and the last trump of 1 Cor 15:52 are associated with blessing whereas the last trumpet of Rev 11:15 is associated with judgement. The trump here could answer to the silver trumpet or trumpets of Numbers 10:2-4. Again there is no definite article here and so it could be a further characteristic of the shout. W.E.Vine states, If, as seems probable, the subject of this threefold description is one great signal from heaven, then the words may be paraphrased: 'with a shout in the archangel's voice, even with the voice of the trump of God.'

It is also suggested that 'the shout' is to the saints of this period, calling them away from this world, 'the voice of the archangel' is to indicate that God is once more taking up Israel and 'the trump of God' indicates that God is once more taking direct dealing with the earth.

"and the dead in Christ shall rise first:" This statement substantiates what Paul stated in verse 15, "we which are alive and remain . . . shall not prevent them which are asleep." 'First' as to the order of things. The apostle uses the word 'dead' here and not the word 'asleep' to emphasise that not even death could break their relationship with Christ and to show that the body has a part in that relationship. We take the expression 'dead in Christ' as indicating believers of the Church period. Nothing is said here of the change of the body that will take place when corruption shall put on incorruption, as that is the subject of 1 Cor 15:51-57.

Verse 17. **"Then we which are alive and remain shall be caught up"** The word translated 'caught up' is translated 'catcheth away' (Matt 13:19), 'take by force' (John 6:15), and 'pluck' (John 10:28) - see also 2 Cor 12:2, 4. The word contains the idea of force exerted and means carried away by force or snatched away. Thus the word Rapture aptly describes what will take place. Again there is no mention of the change that will occur relative to the bodies of the living saints (see 1 Cor 15:53). In that day, in the experience of the living saints the principles that will be working death in their bodies will be utterly destroyed. This event could well be summed up in the words of 2 Cor 5:4, "that mortality might be swallowed up of life" (see Phil 3:20:21). Although 'caught up' indicates rapidity we must point out the expression "In a moment, in the twinkling of an eye" is used in relation to the change of the body and not to being caught up or snatched away (1 Cor 15:52).

"together with them" The living saints together with the dead in Christ who have been raised. There will be a glorious Reunion. For the first time all the saints of the Church will be together. The Church will be complete. The Lord comes to take away His Bride. Caught away together - away out of this earth and the circumstances of earth - away from the coming wrath (1 Thess 1:10 - see also 1 Thess 5:9).

"in the clouds," There are three suggestions as to the meaning of this statement:-

(i) The Shekinah cloud as in Exod 40:34 is in view. Shekinah comes from the Hebrew word 'shaken' meaning to dwell. The cloud was a visible representation of the presence of God amongst His people and of the glory of God (Exod 24:16; Lev 16:2). This Shekinah cloud appeared at the Transfiguration (Matt 17:5) and many believe is mentioned at the Lord's ascension (Acts 1:9). The fact that here the plural is used may not be in keeping with this suggestion.

(ii) These clouds are figurative of groups of believers from different parts of the world caught up to meet the Lord. The fact that the expression is literally 'in clouds' would seem to support this meaning. However appealing this might sound it is unlikely that the body of saints, the Church, will ascend in different groups.

(iii) These are literal clouds. This seems to be the case at the Manifestation of the Lord (Matt 24:30; 26:64).The most likely meaning of this expression is that of the natural clouds.

"to meet the Lord" What a glorious moment to see the One, Whom having not seen we love. The last pain will have been felt, the last tear will have been shed, never more to fail - then we will be able to worship Him as we ought, praise Him with unsinning lips, and serve Him perfectly.

Oh the blessed joy of meeting, all the desert past!
Oh the wondrous words of greeting, He shall speak at last!

"in the air:" The place of meeting - the atmosphere - the very place which is the sphere or domain of Satan (Eph 2:2). Thus the Lord demonstrates His complete and absolute triumph over Satan. No power can prevent that glorious meeting in the Air. Here is the fulfilment of the Lord's promise - "receive you unto myself" (John 14:3).

"and so shall we ever be with the Lord." As a result of this we shall be for ever with the Lord - "that where I am, there ye may be also." (John 14:3).

He and I in that bright glory, One deep joy shall share;
Mine, to be for ever with him, His, that I am there.

Thus at the Lord's coming there will be Resurrection, Rapture, Reunion, Reception and Rest. The intended result of this revelation is to bring comfort to the saints as stated in the next verse. We notice how the title 'Lord' occurs in this section - "the word of the Lord" and "the coming of the Lord" (Verse 15); "the Lord himself" (Verse 16); "to meet the Lord" and "be with the Lord" (Verse 17).

Verse 18. The Result of the Revelation
"Wherefore comfort one another with these words." The apostle now applies the revelation, which he has unfolded, to the circumstances of the Thessalonian believers who were distressed at the death of their fellow believers. This revelation

is the answer to their perplexities. Their fellow believers who had fallen asleep will not miss anything but will share with them the glory of the Lord's coming and kingdom. The imminency of the Lord's coming for His own is intended to be a comfort to every child of God.

CHAPTER 5

Instructional

In the closing verses of Chapter 4 the apostle writes of the Lord's coming to take away His own from this world. Now, in the opening verses of Chapter 5, he writes of the coming judgement on the world in the Day of the Lord. This subject is one of the themes of the Old Testament in contrast to the new revelation in the closing verses of Chapter 4. After writing of the Day of the Lord (verses 1-11) the apostle mentions their responsibility towards their leaders (verses 12-13) and then gives his final exhortations (verses 14-22), before unfolding his desire for them (verses 23-24) and concluding the epistle (verses 25-28). We can divide the chapter into four parts:- Verses 1- 11 The Day of the Lord; Verses 12-22 The Detailed Instructions; Verses 23-24 The Desire and Prayer of Paul; and Verses 25-29 Closing Requests and Benediction.

Verses 1-11 The Day of the Lord

The subject before us indicates that there are solemn events ahead for this world when the Day of the Lord dawns. However this section also brings before us the consummation of salvation for the children of God at the Lord's coming. The section is divided into three parts:- 1. Verses 1-5 The Contrast between the sons of the light and the sons of night, 2. Verses 6-8 The Character which is suitable to the sons of light and Verses 9-11 The Consummation of salvation.

1. Verses 1-5 The Contrast Emphasised

These Thessalonian saints were suffering severe persecution (see 2:14; 3:3-5). False teachers, taking advantage of that persecution, were seeking to convince the saints that the day of the Lord was already present. They were even using at least one letter, on which they had forged Paul's signature, to substantiate their evil teaching (2 Thess 2:2). In these opening verses the apostle is seeking to alleviate their anxiety by reminding them of his teaching. The apostle wrote his second letter to them to assure them that the day of the Lord was not present and that it could not come until the apostasy was fully developed and until the coming of our Lord Jesus Christ and our gathering together unto Him (2 Thess 2).

Verse 1. **"But"** This indicates that a new subject is being introduced. Whereas the subject of chap 4:16-18 has to do with salvation, the subject introduced here has to do with judgement. As we have noted that Chap 4:16-17 can be linked with John 14:1-3 so we note that these opening verses of Chap 5 can be linked with Matt 24.

"of the times and the seasons, brethren," Although both Greek words are translated 'time' and 'season' and are considered as synonyms, they must be distinguished in meaning when used together. The Greek word translated 'times' has the idea of duration (see Matt 25:19; Luke 1:57) and is translated 'while' (John 7:33; 12:35), 'space' (Acts 15:33) and 'season (Acts 19:22; 20:18). It refers to periods of time, whether in the past (Acts 1:21), the present (Acts 1:6) or the future (Acts 3:21) and whether short (Luke 4:5) or long (Acts 13:18). The Greek word translated 'seasons' however refers to the features or characteristics of the different periods of time, such as a period of fruit bearing (Matt 21:41), of temptation (Luke 8:13) and of reaping (Gal 6:9). The two words are only used together here and in Acts 1:7 and generally relate to events on earth and particularly in regard to Israel. The saints of this present period are a heavenly people and should be occupied with things which are above (Col 3:2). We are not suggesting that believers ignore or neglect prophecy but we would emphasise that a knowledge of prophecy is intended to have a practical effect upon our lives now (2 Pet 3:11).

"ye have no need that I write unto you." The apostle and his companions had already instructed the Thessalonians concerning this subject (God's prophetic programme) so there was no need for Paul to write in detail about it. The Church is heavenly in origin and destiny and does not form part of that prophetic programme which deals with events on earth. Thus this present period when the Church is being formed is looked on as a parenthesis and is not envisaged in the Old Testament.

Verse 2. **"For yourselves know perfectly"** The word translated 'perfectly' is also translated 'diligently (Matt 2:8) and 'circumspectly' (Eph 5:15), and means accurately, exactly or precisely. This indicates that Paul and his companions were careful ministers of the Word of God and that the Thessalonian believers had listened intently to that ministry. Thus the Thessalonians had an accurate understanding of this subject. It is important that those who minister do so with care and accuracy, and that those who listen do so with diligence.

"that the day of the Lord" This expression does not refer to a particular day of 24 hours but to a long period of time or programme of events which is yet future. This is one of the great subjects of the Old Testament prophetical books. Although on occasions this expression is used to refer to local events, it is generally prophetic in character. Sometimes the expressions 'that day' (Joel 3:18; Zeph 1:15) and 'the day' (Isaiah 13:13; Ezek 30:18) are used of this period of time. The day of the Lord will be both a time of judgement (Zeph 1:14-18) and a time of blessing (Zeph 3:14-17). It commences with judgement (Isaiah 13:6-18) and includes the great tribulation (Matt 24:21-29), the manifestation of Christ and His triumph over His enemies (Zech 14:1-3; Rev 19:11-21), the restoration of Israel (Isaiah 14:1-4; Ezek 37:12-14; Amos 9:11-15), all the events of the Millennium when Christ will be in the midst of Israel (Zeph 3:11-17) and the passing away of the heavens and the earth (2 Peter 3:10). In these verses the apostle is referring to the commencement of the day of the Lord.

We must distinguish between the day of the Lord and the day of God (2 Peter 3:12), and between the day of the Lord and the day of Christ (Phil 1:10). The day of God refers to the new heavens and the new earth where righteousness dwells - the eternal state (2 Pet 3:12). The day of Christ (also called the day of our Lord Jesus Christ - 1 Cor 1:8, the day of the Lord Jesus - 2 Cor 1:14, and the day of Jesus Christ - Phil 1:6) refers to the events during the Lord's presence with His own (the Church) between the Rapture and the Revelation.

"so cometh as a thief in the night." The idea here is of suddenness and unpreparedness (see Luke 21:34). The Thessalonians knew that the day of the Lord would come suddenly and when least expected. This shows the futility of trying to date fix both the Rapture and the commencement of the day of the Lord. The mention of night could imply the character of dark judgement that will characterise the commencement of the day of the Lord (Zeph 1:15).

Verse 3. **"For when they shall say, Peace and safety;"** Peace here seems to have the thought of freedom from war - being at rest from turmoil. The word translated 'safety' is only used elsewhere in Acts 5:23 and Luke 1:4 (translated 'certainty') and means security. Politicians today are seeking to bring about peace and stability. In a coming day they will think that they have achieve that end and people generally will be deluded into thinking that all is well.

"then sudden destruction cometh upon them," The day of the Lord, when it comes at last, will come suddenly upon those who confidently say, "Peace and safety". It will be dark and dreadful with the judgements of God. The word translated 'destruction' conveys the thought of the ruination of well being, the loss of all that is worth while.

"as travail upon a woman with child;" Here it is neither the woman's knowledge of what is expected or the anticipation of the birth of a child that is in view but the unexpected and unavoidable pangs of labour. The expression is used in the Old

Testament to indicate sorrow, pain and anguish (Isaiah 13:8; Jer 6:24; 13:21).

"and they shall not escape." Here we see the inevitability of judgement and the impossibility of fleeing to safety.

Verse 4. **"But ye, brethren,"** The indication of an essential contrast between believers and the world and between their destiny and the destiny of unbelievers.

"are not in darkness," Not in the moral slumber and ignorance of the world (see Eph 4:18). Here it is the thought of that moral and spiritual darkness which results from being at a distance from God Who is light and Who gives light. It indicates an ignorance of the truth of God and a moral condition that is opposite to the holiness of God. "Here the metaphor of darkness is in harmony with the simile of the thief in the night" (W.E.Vine). The child of God should not be ignorant of the truth of God as it is contained in the Word of God. There should be a diligence in reading and meditating upon the Word of God.

"that that day should overtake you as a thief." In order that you be not overtaken, i.e. the divine purpose is that only the dwellers in darkness be overtaken by the judgements of the Day of the Lord. The word translated 'overtake' means to seize or come upon with hostile intent. The Thessalonian believers had been brought into the light of the gospel and were no longer ignorant of the truth. The day of the Lord will not come upon the believers of this day of grace because they will be removed from the world at the coming of the Lord, before it comes (see Chap 1:10).

Verse 5. **"Ye are all the children of the light, and the children of the day:"** The word translated 'children' is also translated sons (Rom 8:14; Gal 4:6) and sometimes indicate moral characteristics. We were once of the night, in darkness and under the control of the power of darkness but God has worked for us bringing us out of darkness into His marvellous light (Col 1:13; 1 Pet 2:9). God has worked for us in order to sever the ties that once made us morally one with the world. He has forever severed those ties, separating us from the world altogether, making us sons of the light and sons of the day. This truth of separation is one of the oldest truths in the Scriptures. In Genesis 1:4-5 God divided the light from the darkness and called the separated light day. Light and darkness are two separate spheres that can never really meet. Thus the believer should live a separated life for "what communion hath light with darkness" (2 Cor 6:14).

"we are not of the night, nor of darkness." We were once sons of the night, characterised by sin and at a distance from God, dwellers in darkness, but that is no longer true of us. Now we belong to a different environment altogether. Instead of being morally one with the world we are now morally one with God, having been "justified freely by his grace through the redemption that is in Christ Jesus:" (Rom 3:24). God now sees us in Christ without spot or stain. However it is our responsibility to live in keeping with our standing in Christ - we "should live soberly, righteously, and godly, in this present world:" (Titus 2:12).

2. *Verses 6-8 The Character Expected*
These verses emphasize that believers have a responsibility to live as those who are the sons of the light and sons of the day.

Verse 6. **"Therefore"** The apostle now applies the previous verses to show the responsibility of the saints both in a negative and positive way. He unfolds the character that is suitable to those who belong to the light and are of the day - character which is manifested in ways suitable for sons of the light.

"let us not sleep," We note that three times in these verses we have the expression 'let us'. This shows that Paul is associating himself with the Thessalonians in these exhortations. The Greek word translated 'sleep' here is not the same as in Chap 4:13-15 which refers to physical death. Here 'sleep' refers to a moral attitude of carnal indifference and lethargy by the believer both to spiritual things, and to the solemn responsibilities of Christian living. It is a condition of insensibility to divine claims and a conformity to the world. How sad when believers live and act like the world. This condition is not suitable for the sons of the light. We need to examine ourselves and if this is our condition then its high time we awoke out of sleep (Eph 5:14) for the Lord is coming. His coming is imminent.

"as do others;" A contrast between believers and unbelievers (see 4:13). The natural state of unbelievers is sleep (indifference to eternal issues) since they belong to the night and are in darkness.

"but let us watch" Watching is the opposite to sleeping. The word 'watch' indicates vigilance and mental alertness. It means to give attention to spiritual things and to take heed to divine teaching. It also indicates being on one's guard. There is a need for spiritual alertness today because of false teaching (2 Pet 3:17) and we need to be vigilant against the attacks of the enemy (1 Pet 5:8). There is also a need to be vigilant in carrying out the teaching of the Word of God (1 Cor 16:13; 2 Tim 4:5) and we need to be watching for the Lord's coming.

"and be sober." The word 'sober' is in contrast to the word 'drunken' in verse 7 - not intoxicated - not under the influence of that which is detrimental. Believers can be under the influence of worldliness, materialism, pleasure, sport and many other things. Sober here means self-control. It indicates holding one's self on a tight reign - holding one's self under discipline - the discipline of the Word of God. The idea seems to be that of living in the realisation of the solemnity of life and of the seriousness of spiritual things. It is to live in the appreciation of the importance of pleasing God in light of the Lord's imminent return.

Let us not sleep - be Awake; Let us watch - be Alert; Let us be sober - be Aware.

Verse 7. **"For"** Introducing that which belongs to the night.

"they that sleep sleep in the night;" Naturally sleep is associated with the night when darkness covers the land. As sleep is natural during the night so it is natural for the unregenerate to be characterised by careless indifference to God and spiritual things. Spiritually, it is night for the world when gross darkness reigns. Unbelievers are sons of the night and love darkness rather than light (John 3:19). Blinded by the god of this age they have no concern for their eternal destiny and are thus marked by apathy and self-indulgence. The Gospel alone is able to illuminate their darkened minds and to turn them from darkness to light (Acts 26:18; 2 Cor 4:6). Believers were once in darkness but are now in the light and should conduct themselves as children of light (Eph 5:8). For the believer it is now the day of opportunity to serve the Lord Jesus in the gross darkness of the world which continues to reject Him and is opposed to God and His word.

"and they that be drunken are drunken in the night." Generally drunkenness belongs to the night (see Acts 2:15) so that the shame of it can be covered by darkness. The word translated 'drunken' means intoxication and can be used as a metaphor for anything that dulls the spiritual senses (see Isaiah 29:9-10). Men can be intoxicated with pride, pleasure, passion, material advancement and many other things that dull their sense of eternal realities. The world has been intoxicated with evolution, humanism, religion and philosophy. Sadly, believers can become intoxicated with the things of this world robbing them of spiritual desires, true satisfaction and spiritual growth. As sons of the day, believers should, "walk honestly, as in the day; not in rioting and drunkenness, not in chambering and wantonness, not in strife and envying. But put ye on the Lord Jesus Christ, and make not provision for the flesh, to fulfil the lusts thereof." (Rom 13:13).

Verse 8. **"But let us, who are of the day,"** This indicates a contrast to the activities of the night. As sons of the day, believers are to walk in the light (Eph 5:8; 1 John 1:7).

"be sober," The mention of the word 'sober' again emphasises what is expected of the sons of the day in contrast to the intoxication mentioned in verse 7. Sobriety involves avoiding all excesses and the judging of self in the light of the Word of God. The thought of watchfulness and sobriety presents the figure of a soldier on guard and thus the need of armour - the armour of faith, love and hope. As the sons of light, believers must put on the armour of light (Rom 13:12).

"putting on" The thought here is of clothing one's self as with a garment. The tense here indicates putting the armour on once and for all - "putting the armour on and keeping it on" (W.E.Vine). Thus the believer must always wear the armour expecting an attack at any time. In Eph 6 we have, "the whole armour" but here only two articles are mentioned for the protection of the heart and the head - the affections and the mind.

"the breastplate of faith and love;" In Eph 6:14 we have the breastplate of righteousness. There the protection of our affection is resting in what we are in Christ, i.e. our righteous standing in Christ. Here it is the breastplate of faith and love - a two sided breastplate. One has suggested faith on the outside and love on the inside. Faith that has its roots in the unseen and that now lays hold upon eternal realities, standing firmly upon the truth of God. Love - in the enjoyment of the love of Christ and the love of God (Rom 8:35-39; Gal 2:20). It is faith and love together for "faith worketh by love" (Gal 5:6). I believe God and I am loved of God - these two things assure the believer that he/she is of the day and not of the night.

"and for an helmet, the hope of salvation." In Eph 6:17 we have the helmet of salvation. Salvation is viewed in different aspects in the Scriptures. It is viewed as being past in Eph 2:8, as being present in 1 Cor 1:18 and as being future in Rom 5:9. In Eph 6:17 it is present salvation that is in view, i.e. salvation possessed. The believer is viewed as being in the heavenlies standing in the inheritance. The knowledge of this will keep the believer's mind steady and prevent doubts and despondency. Here the helmet is the hope of salvation, i.e. full salvation when the Lord comes. It is salvation in all its fullness - the final deliverance, at the rapture, from all that mars and distresses which involves a changed body (See Eph 1:14; Phil 3:21) and the eradication of the flesh. It is a certain hope which could be realised at any moment. This hope is certain because it is founded upon Christ and His word. The knowledge of the imminent return of Christ will protect the mind from discouragement and disappointments.

3. Verses 9-11 The Consummation Envisaged

The consummation of salvation is indicated in the expression, 'that we should live together with him' (Verse 10) and these verses emphasize the certainty of that consummation.

Verse 9. **"For"** Either the explanation of 'the hope of salvation' or a further reason for putting on the armour.

"God hath not appointed us to wrath," The apostle has mentioned two companies, the sons of the night and their destruction and the sons of the day and their salvation. He now introduces divine appointment in relation to the latter. First he mentions the negative side of this appointment and then the positive side. Wrath, here, has reference to the judgement to be poured out upon the earth at the beginning of the 'day of the Lord' (see Rev 6:16-17; 15:1, 7: 16:1). The Sovereign appointment of God is that we escape the wrath to come (see chap 1:10). The Church will not go through the great tribulation of that coming day.

"but to obtain salvation" In verses 9-10 we have two fundamental facts that emphasize the sure consummation of our salvation - complete salvation. Here is the first fundamental fact - the Sovereign appointment of God. The Greek word translated 'obtain' means to acquire or possess (see Eph 1:14 "possession" and 1 Peter 2:9 "peculiar"). It is the possessing of salvation in all its completeness. God, has, in His sovereignty, appointed the end for the sons of the light. That end is sure. Thus we have the sure consummation of life with Christ, based upon the Sovereignty of God.

"by our Lord Jesus Christ," Just as every other aspect of salvation is through our blessed Lord and Saviour so the consummation of our salvation is through Him, i.e. by his coming for us as unfolded in chap 4:16-17.

Verse 10. **"Who died for us,"** Here is the second fundamental fact - the Sacrificial death of the Lord Jesus Christ. The sure consummation of our salvation is based upon the infinite value of the death of our blessed Saviour on the cross. The finished work of the Lord Jesus Christ is the guarantee for every believer of obtaining salvation in all its fullness.

"that, whether we wake or sleep," There are two ways to look at this expression:-

1) Some feel that 'wake or sleep' refers to the two companies of believers mentioned in chap 4:16-17 - those who are alive and remain and the dead in Christ. It has been pointed out that there will be these two classes at the consummation of salvation when the Lord comes. So that whether we are alive or have died at the Lord's coming we shall live together with Him. This would be a further encouragement to the Thessalonians who were anxious concerning their fellow believers who had fallen asleep (see Chap 4:13-14). Those who take this view feel that this enhances the exhortations of verses 6-8 whereas to take sleep in an ethical way would retract from the exhortation.

2) Others feel that 'wake or sleep' refers to the vigilance and indifference of verse 6, i.e. to spiritual alertness or carnal indifference. The Greek word translated 'wake' is never used of being alive but is translated watch in verse 6 and the Greek word translated 'sleep' is a different word to the one translated 'sleep' in Chap 4:13-14 but is the word translated sleep in verses 6-7. So that whatever our spiritual condition now, at the Lord's coming we shall live together with Him. The consummation of our salvation does not depend upon our spiritual condition but upon the two fundamental facts already mentioned. However this does not give licence to carnal indifference to spiritual things as this will be taken into account at the Judgement Seat of Christ (2 Cor 5:10).

Whichever view we accept, the expression emphasises that every genuine child of God will live together with him as stated in the next expression.

"we should live together with him." To live indicates eternal life in its fullness which necessitates the change of 1 Cor 15:51 and takes place at the rapture (see Phil 3:20-21). The moral change fitting us to enjoy the presence of God took place when we trusted Christ. However a physical change is necessary to enter into the fullness of life eternal, to inherit the kingdom of God (1 Cor 15:50), i.e. the future and heavenly aspect of the kingdom. Then death will be swallowed up in victory (1 Cor 15:54) and mortality will be swallowed up of life (2 Cor 5:4). Together with Him links with the expression 'so shall we ever be with the Lord' (chap 4:17).

Verse 11. **"Wherefore comfort yourselves together,"** Here we have the conclusion of the passage. For 'comfort' see 'exhort' chap 4:1 and 'comfort' see chap 4:18. The word translated 'together' here has the thought of reciprocation and is translated 'one another' in chap 3:12; 4:9, 18. The thought is that of consoling or exhorting each other.

"and edify one another," The word translated 'edify', "expresses the strengthening effect of teaching, 1 Cor 14:3, and example, 10:23, upon oneself, and upon others, 14:4, whether for good, 2 Cor 10:8, or for evil, 1 Cor 8:10, 'emboldened' (Hogg & Vine). It has the thought of building up spiritually by means of teaching. Here we have the responsibility of every believer to seek the spiritual well being of fellow believers. In the light of the sure consummation of our salvation we should seek to be a spiritual help to other saints through the Word of God and by example. One has stated, "Because we will live together with Him then, we should live together with one another co-operatively now."

"even as also ye do." The Thessalonians were already practising what the apostle was exhorting them to do (see Chap 4:10). Here is Paul's recognition and commendation of this fact which is intended to encourage them in this practice. Are we, like the Thessalonians, practising the teaching of the Word of God?

Verses 12-22 The Detailed Instructions

The closing part of the epistle contains various exhortations. Although the Thessalonian believers had been set forth as an example to others (chap 1:7) they were not exempt from the need of exhortation. Whatever our spiritual condition, there is always room for improvement and thus the need for exhortation. The passage can be divided into two parts:- Verses 12-13 The Recognition of Leaders and Verses 14-22 Various Exhortations

1. Verses 12-13 The Recognition of Leaders

Verse 12. **"And we beseech you, brethren,"** The apostle now passes from the saints' responsibility to comfort and edify each other, to the recognition of leaders in their midst. He again appeals to them as brethren, indicating his relationship with them and expressing his love for them. The word 'beseech' means to ask or request. Here it is a strong request to all the saints, apart from their leaders, in light of the fact that some were unruly (Verse 4).

"to know them which labour among you," The word translated 'to know' means "to recognise and acknowledge, to appreciate and value; a purely spiritual exercise possible only to spiritual persons" (Hogg & Vine). The idea would not only be one of recognition but also of respect. The word translated 'labour' means to labour with wearisome toil. It indicates diligence - spending time and energy for the benefit of the saints. Thus the leaders are recognised by their labours. They are not apart from the saints but among the saints, being themselves saints. They toil in the midst of the saints for the spiritual well being of the saints (see 1 Tim 5:17).

"and are over you" The Greek word translated 'over' means 'to put or stand before' and is elsewhere translated 'rule' (Rom 12:8; 1 Tim 3:4, 5, 12; 5:17) and 'maintain' (Tit 3:8, 14). The idea here is of presiding over. This verse, as well as other scriptures, indicates a plurality of leaders in each local assembly. Both one man and any man rule in an assembly are foreign to the teaching of the New Testament. We suggest that there are six words or terms used of these leaders:-

(i) Elders (Acts 20:17; 1 Tim 5:17) - their worth. This indicates their spiritual maturity and that they are spiritual men with experience and ability.

(ii) Overseers (also called Bishops - Acts 20:28; Phil 1:1; 1 Tim 3:1-2) - their work. The Greek word signifies visitation, and then inspection. The idea is that of oversight (1 Pet 5:2) indicating spiritual discernment to meet the spiritual needs of the saints.

(iii) Leaders or Guides (Heb 13:7, 17 "rule over you" - your guides) - their walk. The Greek word means 'to lead or to go before'. It indicates that they lead or guide not only by instruction but also by example. They practice what they preach.

(iv) Shepherds (1 Pet 5:2 "feed" - to shepherd) - their watchfulness. They are under shepherds taking character from the Chief Shepherd (1 Pet 5:4) and watching over the flock - guarding and feeding the sheep.

(v) Steersmen (1 Cor 12:28 "governments") - their wisdom. The Greek word means 'to steer'. It carries the idea of piloting safely the saints through difficult times. They steer the assembly through treacherous waters to prevent shipwreck of the collective testimony.

(vi) Rulers (1 Thess 5:12) - their ways. We have noted that the Greek word is translated 'rule' and 'maintain'. They maintain divine principles in the assembly by directing the saints to the Word of God. They preside over the saints according to the Word of God and thus maintain the principles of gathering.

"in the Lord," This indicates that their authority has its origin in the Lord and that their rule is in keeping with His Word. It is evident from Acts 20:28 that spiritual leaders are divinely appointed.

"and admonish you;" The word translated 'admonish' is translated 'warn' in verse 14. It means to caution, to put in mind - to warn or correct by instruction. "The stress is upon influencing not merely the intellect but the will and disposition" (Kittel).

Verse 13. **"And to esteem them very highly in love"** Esteem is to consider, to reckon or to regard. Here it has the idea of honouring or respecting. The word translated 'very highly' means exceeding abundantly, indicating the intensity of the esteem. It means to give them a high place in one's estimation. The motive for such esteem should be love. Love should govern the attitude of all the saints towards their spiritual leaders. Love is the antidote against any resentment that may arise because of admonition.

"for their work's sake." The high estimation is not because of their personality but because of their work. Their labour, out of love, for the saints deserves the response of loving regard and esteem (see Phil 2:29-30). They are to be recognised by their labour and to be esteemed in love because of their work.

"And be at peace among yourselves." The Greek word translated 'be at peace' only occurs elsewhere in Mark 9:50 (have peace), Rom 12:18 (live peaceably) and 2 Cor 13:11 (live in peace). The word can indicate both a state and an attitude. The idea hear is that of exercising peace - be a peacemaker and not a trouble maker. Harmony in the assembly is essential to the testimony of the assembly. The assembly cannot be torn by strife and carnality without the loss of effective testimony. There is a danger of resentment, by some of the saints, to one or more of the leaders. This could lead to unrest and division in the assembly. Peaceful and loving submission to spiritual leaders without party spirit is essential for the harmony of the assembly.

Verses 14-22 Various Exhortation

Verse 14. **"Now we exhort you, brethren,"** Some suggest that these exhortations are addressed to the leaders mentioned in the previous verses, because of the first exhortation in regard to the unruly, and that the term 'brethren' is used in this limited way. Others state that the apostle is still addressing all the saints and the term 'brethren' is all inclusive, as on other occasions. Thus every believer is to seek the good of the company. The word translated 'exhort' is translated 'comfort' in verse 11 and has the thought of addressing a person or persons in order to produce an effect, i.e urging them to act for the benefit of all. Although the exhortations are addressed to all the saints, some of them seem to be the particular responsibility of the leaders.

"warn them that are unruly," For the word 'warn' see 'admonish' in verse 12. The word translated 'unruly' only occurs here in the New Testament and is a military term meaning those out of rank. The verb only occurs in 2 Thess 3:7 (disorderly) and the adverb only occurs in 2 Thess 3:6, 11 (disorderly). The passage in 2 Thess 3 where both the verb and adverb occurs indicate that idleness is in view. There were some among the Thessalonian believers who would not work for a living but who relied upon others to provide for them (see Chap 4:11). Those in view are not those who cannot work or who are out of work through no fault of their own, but those who will not work or who have no desire to work. It is evident that idleness characterised some even when Paul was among them (2 Thess 3:10). Idleness manifests a selfish attitude with a disregard for others and is contrary to the teaching of the Word of God (see Acts 20:35; 2 Thess 3:6). Laziness is a blight on the testimony and spiritual leaders have the responsibility to admonish such that they may be brought back into rank, into harmony with the rest of the saints.

"comfort the feebleminded," The word translated 'comfort' is different to the one in verse 11, the only distinction, it seems, being that this word is never used directly of God's comfort. Here the idea is that of encouragement as well as of comfort. The word translated 'feebleminded' comes from two words meaning 'small' and 'soul or spirit', thus meaning small souled, low spirited or faint hearted. It refers to those who are discouraged or despondent. This could be the result of the persecution they were enduring, or because of the loss of loved ones, or because of their sensitivity to failure. As such they needed comforting words and encouragement along the pathway of faith. How needful to pass on a kind and comforting word to fellow believers and to encourage them along life's journey.

"support the weak," The word translated 'support' is only found elsewhere in Matt 6:24; Luke 16:13 (hold to) and Titus 1:9 (holding fast) and means to keep hold of someone or something. In Matt 6:24 and Luke 16:13 the idea is of cleaving to one master and in Titus 1:9 it has the idea of keeping hold of the faithful word, the Word of God. Here the idea is that of keeping hold of persons in the sense of supporting them. The word 'weak' refers to those who are spiritually weak through lack of knowledge, lack of understanding or lack of courage. They are not to be despised but supported, sustained and assisted (see Rom 14:1-3; 15:1; 1 Cor 8:9-11). They need the tender care of the shepherds of the flock.

"be patient toward all men." The word translated 'patient' is used of the longsuffering character of love (1 Cor 13:4), of the longsuffering of God (2 Pet 3:9) and is one of the parts of the fruit of the Spirit (Gal 5:22-23). "It is that quality of self-restraint in the face of provocation which does not hastily retaliate" (Hogg & Vine). Not only the leaders but all the saints should exercise forbearance towards others under the varying circumstances and conditions of life. This is only possible because of the indwelling Spirit and only actual when we allow the Spirit to govern and control our lives.

Verse 15. **"See that none render evil for evil unto any man;"** The word 'see' suggests a warning since this practice might take them unawares. The believer must take care not to drift into the attitude of retaliation which is evident in the world. The combination of the 2nd and 3rd persons in this statement implies that the whole company is responsible for the conduct of each individual. The idea in the expression is, "see to it that not one of you renders to anyone evil for evil". The word translated 'render' means to give back, to repay or to recompense (see Rom 12:17; 1 Pet 3:9). The revengeful spirit is not in keeping with the patience mentioned in verse 14, is not in keeping with the example of Christ (1 Pet 2:21-23) and is contrary to the teaching of the Lord (Luke 6:27-31; see also Prov 20:22).

"but ever follow that which is good," This is in contrast to the previous statement and the word translated 'ever' indicates that this should be the rule of the believer's life. The word translated 'follow' means to pursue eagerly or to follow zealously (see Phil 3:12). Good is in contrast to evil and could either refer to that which is good in itself or to that which is good to others. Here the context indicates that it is the latter. It should be the norm of Christian living to seek the well being of others. Every believer should be "zealous of good works" (Titus 2:14; See also Matt 5:16).

"both among yourselves," Christians have a special relationship to each other and therefore should especially seek the welfare and benefit of each other (see Gal 6:10; James 2:15-17).

"and to all men." The pursuit of good should be at all times, in all places, on all occasions and to all men - "be careful to maintain good works. These things are good and profitable unto men." (Titus 3:8).

Verse 16. **"Rejoice evermore."** Whereas the previous exhortations are in relation to others the exhortations in verses 16-18 are personal, in relation to themselves. The word translated 'rejoice' is used as a greeting in Acts 15:23; 23:26 and James 1:1, where it is translated 'greeting' (see also hail in Luke 1:28), and as a salutation in 2 Cor 13:11 (farewell). The word is translated 'joy' in Chap 3:9 and means to be glad, to be delighted or to be joyful. This joy or gladness is from within and does not depend upon outward conditions or circumstances. The Thessalonian saints were passing through severe persecution yet are exhorted to rejoice. This is in keeping with the Lord's teaching in Matt 5:12 (see 1 Peter 1:6) - "But rejoice, inasmuch as ye are partakers of Christ's suffering; that, when his glory shall be revealed, ye may be glad also with exceeding joy" (1 Peter 4:13). The tense here indicates a continual rejoicing. We should rejoice in hope (Rom 12:12) and in the Lord (Phil 4:4) not allowing any trials, problems or difficulties to rob us of the joy of the Lord. We, who are Christians should, above all others, be a rejoicing people considering the rich blessings God has abundantly bestowed upon us and the bright future that is before us. Rejoicing instead of retaliating and rejoicing in the pursuit of that which is good is the link with the previous verse.

Verse 17. **"Pray without ceasing."** The word translated 'pray' is the more general and comprehensive term containing various aspects of addressing God, and can be silent or audible. Prayer in general is an expression of dependence upon God and an evidence of need. It is an acknowledgement of inability and weakness as to one's self but of confidence in the ability and power of God. Appreciation of our own weakness drives us to seek God and to call upon Him for His help. Involved in prayer is an appreciation of His worth and an acceptance of His will. There is always a need for prayer - "men ought always to pray, and not faint;" (Luke 18:1). This exercise of prayer seems to be one of the most neglected activities among the people of God and yet it is vital to the Christian life. The believer is to pray in faith, i.e. believing and not doubting (Matt 21:22; James 1:6). Prayer should also be in the power of the indwelling Spirit - engendered and energised by the Spirit (Eph 6:18; Jude 20). Christians need the help of the gracious Spirit of God in their prayer life (see Rom 8:26). There is also the need for vigilance in prayer guarding the mind against fleshly intrusion and persevering against the powers of darkness (Eph 6:18). Watching is to attend constantly to prayer involving spiritual alertness to all that would distract from fervent prayer (see Col 4:2). The word translated 'without ceasing' only occurs elsewhere in the New Testament in 1:3; 2:13 and Rom 1:9, and means without omission, unceasingly or constantly recurring. The Christian should continue in prayer (Rom 12:12) making it a priority in life. There are many hindrances to prayer and thus the exhortation here, showing the need for diligence. In the Christian life there is a need for constant communion with God and for continually being in the spirit of prayer. Prayer is both the cause and the outcome of the rejoicing mentioned in the previous expression.

Verse 18. **"In every thing give thanks:"** The word translated 'everything' means in every condition, every circumstance or every matter even in times of trial and affliction. The word translated 'give thanks' means to be grateful or to express gratitude. Thanksgiving for the privilege and opportunities of prayer as well as for answered prayer would be the link with the previous statement. Redemption has placed the believer in a position of obligation to God for all that He has done and for all that He has bountifully bestowed - "Giving thanks unto the Father, which hath made us meet to be partakers of the inheritance of the saints in light:" (Col 1:12). There should be constant thanksgiving for past guidance and mercies bestowed, for present help and blessings received and for the assurance of future glory. Giving thanks in every circumstance is not always easy, particularly in adverse circumstances and when things seem to go wrong. However this is God's intention for us.

"for this is the will of God" Although grammatically this expression could refer only to the giving of thanks many consider it applies to the three exportations of verses 16-18 - "the commandments immediately proceeding these words are so closely associated in form and idea, that it seems best to understand what follows to refer to all three and not merely to the last of them" (Hogg & Vine). The word translated 'will' means purpose, design or desire and indicates here God's intention for the saints, which includes liberality in giving (2 Cor 8:5), practical sanctification (1 Thess 4:3), submission to governments (1 Pet 2:13-16) as well as thanksgiving in every circumstance of life.

"in Christ Jesus" Two things could be suggested in this expression:- (i) That the Lord not only taught His disciples to rejoice, to pray and to give thanks (Matt 5:12; 6:6-13; 11:25), but was Himself the perfect example in these things for them to follow; (ii) That the power for the saints to carry out the will of God is found in Him (Phil 2:13; 4:13).

"concerning you." This indicates that it is the responsibility of believers not only to have an understanding of the will of god (Eph 5:17) but also to practice the will of God (1 Peter 4:2), doing it from the heart (Eph 6:6). Are we fulfilling our responsibilities?

Verse 19. **"Quench not the Spirit."** The word translated 'quench' means to put out, to extinguish or to stifle and is used in relation to fire whether literal (Heb 11:34) or metaphorical (Eph 6:16). The tense used here along with the negative indicates 'stop continually stifling the Spirit'. Since no man can extinguish the Person of the Spirit the expression must be figurative of the operations or gifts of the Spirit in assembly gatherings - "do not prevent or obstruct the manifestations of the Holy Spirit's power in others" (Hogg & Vine). One man ministry would be a hindrance to the operations of the Spirit and a quenching of the gifts of the Spirit. Any, or every, man ministry would also lead to a stifling of the God given gifts and hinder the control of the Spirit in the gathering of the saints. The use of spiritual gift through fleshly impulse is detrimental to the operations of the gracious Spirit of God and self assertion or human organisation can quench the Spirit, resulting in the loss of spiritual power and blessing. Harshness and unwarranted criticism of younger brethren could hinder them in exercising the gifts they may have and would thus be stifling those gifts. Divine order in the assembly can only be maintained and the saints spiritually enriched and blessed through the presidency and power of the Holy Spirit.

Verse 20. **"Despise not prophesyings."** The word translated 'despise' means to treat with contempt or scorn, to make of no account. It is translated ' set at naught' when used of men's attitude towards the Lord Jesus Christ (Luke 23:11; Acts 4:11). It seems that there was a tendency in Thessalonica to minimise the gift of prophesy which should have been sought after (1 Cor 14:1). This could have been the result of over emphasising the miraculous gifts such as tongues (see 1 Cor 14:5), or a reluctance to accept prophesy because of false prophets (Acts 13:6; 1John 4:1). We must remember that these gifts (1 Cor 12:8-11) were in use when this epistle was written but were later withdrawn when they had completed the purpose for which they were given. They were given for the authentication and inauguration of the new revelation now contained in the New Testament. Once that revelation was complete they were no longer needed. Before the revelation was complete prophets received direct revelations from God for the edification, encouragement and comfort of the saints. Thus to despise these prophesyings was to rob themselves of that instruction and encouragement that was needed for their spiritual development. The teacher has now taken the place of the prophet and he gleans from the Word of God, with the help of the Spirit of God, to edify and encourage the saints. This ministry, given in the power of the Spirit, must not be despised but allowed to affect one's life.

Verse 21. **"Prove all things;"** The word translated 'prove' is translated both 'allow' and 'try' in chap 2:4 and means to prove or approve by putting to the test (1 Cor 3:13 "the fire shall <u>try</u> every man's work"; 1 Cor 11:28 "let a man <u>examine</u> himself"). It means to approve only after weighing things up carefully. Although the prophesyings of the previous verse are in view, the expression 'all things' embraces much more. Believers must not be easily swayed but must test all by the Word of God, placing all things alongside the claims and character of God. The same thought is found in 1 John 4:1 "Beloved, believe not every spirit, but try the spirits whether they are of God: because many false prophets are gone out into the world". We are to be like the Bereans who "searched the scriptures daily, whether those things were so" (Acts 17:11).

"hold fast that which is good." The word translated 'good' indicates that which is intrinsically good and means sterling, virtuous, excellent, beautiful. It is used here to describe that which has been proved to be the truth in contrast to error. It is used in 2 Tim 1:14 of the truth imparted to Timothy which he was to protect and maintain. What is called 'good' here is designated 'sound' in the pastoral epistles (1 Tim 1:10; 2 Tim 1:13; 4:3; Tit 1:9;2:1). Although both words describe the essential character of the truth or Word of God they also indicate the effect of that truth upon the saints. Thus here the truth has a beneficial affect upon the believer who holds that truth firmly. The truth is to be held firmly not only in the mind but also in a practical way.

Verse 22. **"Abstain from all appearance of evil."** The word translated 'abstain' means to refrain or to keep one's self back from something (see chap 4:3) - to hold one's self back from all appearance of evil. The word translated 'appearance' has to do with both vision and manner. The word 'evil' could be taken either as an adjective or as a noun (Ellicott; Morris), i.e. either all evil appearance or every kind of evil. Thus two ideas are suggested:-

(i) The exhortation would be don't do anything that could give the appearance of evil. Avoid all that would appear to be evil, although in itself it is not evil, to safeguard one's Christian testimony (see Rom 14:16). It means to refrain from anything that would cause suspicion of evil in the minds of others. It is very important that the believer's manner of life does not either stumble fellow believers or convey a wrong impression to unbelievers, but enhances his/her Christian testimony.

(ii) The exhortation would be to hold one's self back from every kind of evil. The word translated 'evil' is different from the one in verse 15. The word in verse 15 has the thought of evil in character or in itself whereas the thought here is that of evil in its influence and effect. Here evil is in contrast to what is good in the previous expression and indicates that false prophecy and evil teaching is included in the word. The expression is therefore the negative side of 'hold fast that which is good'. Although evil teaching is included in the word it embraces every kind of evil, whether doctrinal or moral, as the word 'all' indicates.

Although the former idea is true and it is true that believers should be careful as to deportment, it is the latter idea that is in keeping with the context. To hold divine truth firmly will inevitably result in holiness of life but to imbibe evil teaching will inevitably result in evil practice. With all forms of evil increasing today we need to take heed to this timely exhortation. The pressure upon believers to conform to this evil age seems to be increasing. It is therefore vital for each saint to stand firmly upon the truth of God keeping one's self from every kind of evil.

Verses 23-24 The Desire and Prayer of Paul
Verse 23. The apostle now expresses his desire and prayer for the Thessalonian saints knowing that, without the power of God, they would not be able to carry out the exhortations of the previous verses. His pray is short but comprehensive.

"And the very God of peace" the word translated 'peace' signifies prosperity whether spiritually or materially. It also has the idea of being joined in harmony and of a state of well being. The lovely title 'the God of peace' is only used five times in the New Testament. In Rom 15:33 it is used in relation to the saints access in prayer and is in contrast to the implied danger of verse 31; In Rom 16:20 it is used in the promise to encourage the saints in view of those who would disturb their peace and harmony; in Phil 4:9 it is used to denote that God is the source of true peace and that the saints' enjoyment of the peace He bestows depends upon their obedience; in Heb 13:20 it is linked with the perfecting of the saints; and here it is associated with sanctification and is used in contrast to the false peace of verse 3.

"sanctify you wholly;" The word translated 'wholly' only occurs here in the New Testament and means through and through. Thus the expression indicates total sanctification. The ground of peace is the total sanctification of the saints by the God of peace. Divine power alone is sufficient to perfect the work of sanctification in the saints. The apostle seems to have in mind the consummation of sanctification at the Lord's coming. However the practical side here is that of the saints living in the good of the sanctifying power of the God of peace.

"and I pray God your whole spirit and soul and body" Sanctification touches the whole person which is described here as spirit, soul and body. Man is tripartite and thus the prayer of the apostle embraces every faculty of the spirit, soul and body, no part is excluded. One has suggested the following:- The spirit being free from anything that would hinder worship or enjoyment of fellowship with God; the soul free from anything that would defile the emotions and thoughts; and the body free from defiling and unrighteous actions. The word translated 'whole' is only found elsewhere in Jam 1:4 (entire) and means complete in extent or part. It has the idea of being sound or whole in every respect.

"be preserved blameless" The word translated 'preserved' is mainly translated keep or kept (Eph 4:3; 2 Tim 4:7) and means to guard, to watch over or to keep safely. It is singular here although the subject is spirit, soul and body emphasising that the whole person is in view. "The tense regards the continuous preservation of the believer as a single, complete act, without reference to the time occupied in its accomplishment" (W.E.Vine). The word translated 'blameless' is only found elsewhere in chap 2:10 (unblameably) and means faultless - no legitimate cause for censure or blame.

"unto the coming of our Lord Jesus Christ." The Greek proposition translated "unto" is 'en' which generally means "in" and the Greek word 'parousia' is translated "coming" (see 2:19; 3:13; 4:15) - in the coming or presence of our Lord Jesus Christ. Some state that the Judgement Seat is in view here but we feel that the consummation of salvation is indicated. By this we mean the consummation of the work of sanctification and the completeness of salvation. However, we would acknowledge the believer's responsibility to live now in the light of that coming day.

Verse 24. **"Faithful is he that calleth you,"** The apostle now expresses confidence in the fulfilment of his prayer because of the faithfulness of God. Paul has "assurance from God's faithfulness that it will be so" (Alford). The word translated 'faithful' means trustworthy and reliable. God is always true to

His word and calling, and ever acts in keeping with His own character and nature (2 Thess 3:3). The stress is upon the character of the One who calls rather than upon the calling. Since God is absolutely true to His calling and promise He will never fail.

"who also will do it." The word 'also' indicates that God not only calls believers to complete sanctification and salvation but that He Himself will accomplish this in them. God in His faithfulness will confirm every saint right to the end of the pathway so that they will be blameless in that coming day (1 Cor 1:8) and will be "presented faultless before the presence of his glory with exceeding joy" (Jude 24). We have not been left, in our weakness and frailty, to ourselves but have the wondrous assurance of eternal security and future blessedness that is given in this verse.

Verses 25-28 Closing Requests and Benediction
Verse 25. **"Brethren pray for us."** In the previous verses the apostle has been dealing with the needs of the Thessalonians but he now expresses his own need. Paul is deeply conscious of the value and power of prayer (Phil 1:19; Philemon 22), thus he requests prayer on his behalf (Col 4:3; 2 Thess 3:1-2). At the commencement of the epistle he had assured the Thessalonian saints of his prayer for them, now at the close of the epistle he desires their prayers. Both the saints and the servants needed the prayers of each other. In using the term 'brethren' he is appealing to the bonds that bind them together. They were in a common bond, they were on common ground and they had a common need. We need the prayers of each other as we journey along the pilgrim pathway.

Verse 26. **"Greet all the brethren"** The word translated 'greet' means to welcome, to salute (2 Tim 4:19), to enfold or embrace (Heb 11:13). It indicates warmth of feeling, respect and recognition. The greeting or salutation was to be on the apostle's behalf to all the brethren, i.e. to all the saints in the assembly at Thessalonica. In other epistles Paul sends greetings on the behalf of others, he sends his greetings to specified believers and he exhorts the saints to greet each other (Rom 16; 1 Cor 16).

"with an holy kiss." In different countries and cultures there are various forms of greeting. The kiss was the form of greeting then as it is in many eastern countries today whereas here, and in many other countries, it is hand shaking. However, whatever the form, we have here, in principle, the way believers should greet each other. The word 'holy' indicates purity of motive, thought and attitude in the greeting. The word 'kiss' indicates the presence of love and affection in the greeting. Holiness adds sanctity to the greeting while love adds warmth to the greeting. Greetings should be with the heart and in purity, free from anything that is inconsistent with our spiritual relationship. All greetings among the saints should be in transparency being free from both partiality and hypocrisy.

Verse 27. **"I charge you"** The use of the personal pronoun 'I' here indicates the importance of the charge that follows. The word translated 'charge' is only found elsewhere in Mark 5:7 and Acts 19:13 where it is translated 'adjure'. It means to solemnly enjoin or implore, to put under the obligation of a solemn oath. The charge is made to those who would receive the epistle - the elders.

"by the Lord" This expression was to exercise the conscience of the recipients and to indicate the authority behind the charge. The charge was made in the authority of the One who was Lord in and over the assembly.

"that this epistle be read" Paul, being hindered from being at Thessalonica, wrote this epistle to the assembly in which he gives instruction, exhortation and admonition to all and thus it was intended for public reading. The epistle was in fact the inspired word of God to all the saints. It was indeed God speaking to them for their spiritual well being. How important for us to appreciate that God speaks to us through His word for our instruction and benefit. The Holy Spirit is the Author and life of the scriptures - "words which ....the Holy Ghost teacheth"

(1 Cor 2:13 - see also 2 Tim 3:16-17). How solemn it is to treat the Word of God lightly.

"unto all the holy brethren." The epistle was for all in the assembly not for a select few or only for a certain section. The word 'brethren' would again speak of spiritual relationship which included every believer in the assembly. No one was exempt from the teaching of the epistle. This charge seems to indicate that the assembly should meet specially for the reading of this epistle. The teaching of the Word of God is for every child of God.

Verse 28. **"The grace of our Lord Jesus Christ be with you. Amen."** The closing benediction is a token of every epistle of Paul's (2 Thess 3:17-18). Grace is the unmerited favour of God which bestows bountifully His blessing and which would enable them to carry out the teaching and exhortations of the epistle (see 1:1). We need grace to live for God and to faithfully serve Him. We need grace to carry out the teaching of His word for his pleasure and glory and that grace is available to every child of God. This is the apostle's desire at the close of the epistle. As in most of his benedictions Paul uses the full title our 'Lord Jesus Christ'. Having given his benediction the apostle closes with 'Amen' - let it be so.

2 Thessalonians

The Author of the Epistle
There is little challenge as to Paul being the author because the style is, without question, Pauline. The reference to a former letter (2.15) to the same company substantiates this as does the signature at the close of the epistle (3.17).

The Place and Time of Writing
The opening salutation of the epistle proves that Silas and Timothy were with Paul when he wrote it (1.1). The last recorded occasion when all three were together was at Corinth when Silas and Timothy returned from Macedonia (Acts 18.1-5, see also verse 18). Thus Corinth was where both epistles to the Thessalonians were written. It is generally accepted that this epistle was written some months after the first.

The Purpose of the Epistle
Reports from Thessalonica, received after the first epistle had been sent, caused the apostle to write this second epistle. These reports contained at least three predominant elements:- 1. That the persecution was not only continuing, but seemed to be more intense (1.4); 2. That the enemy was now seeking to undermine the truth and shake the confidence of the saints (2.2); 3. That there was still a disorderly faction in the assembly (3.6). These three elements are seen in the three chapters of this second epistle. Thus Chapter 1 deals with the Problem of the Persecution, Chapter 2 with the Problem of Pernicious Teaching using the persecution as a basis and Chapter 3 with the Problem of the Practice, of some in the assembly, which needed rebuke. The purpose of the epistle was therefore to Encourage the Saints in the midst of persecution, to Educate the Saints about the day of the Lord and to Exhort the Saints in relation to their behaviour. Whereas the first epistle brings before us the rapture, the second

epistle brings before us the revelation of Christ. In chapter 1 the apostle comforts and encourages the saints, in chapter 2 he cautions and then explains the events of the day of the Lord and in chapter 3 he commands and exhorts them.

The Division of the Epistle

Chapter 1	The Day of the Lord and Vindication - Promotional.
Verses 1-2	The Introduction.
Verses 3-5	The Increase in the Saints.
Verses 6-10	The Intervention of God.
Verses 11-12	The Intercession of Paul.

Chapter 2	The Day of the Lord and Explanation - Prophetical.
Verses 1-12	Concerning the Day of the Lord.
Verses 1-4	Paul Beseeches the Saints.
Verses 5-12	Paul Reminds the Saints.
Verses 13-17	Concerning the Thessalonians.
Verses 13-15	Paul gives Thanks for the Saints.
Verses 16-17	Paul Commends the Saints to God.

Chapter 3	The Day of the Lord and Application - Practical.
Verses 1-2	Paul's Call or Request to the Saints.
Verses 3-5	Paul's Confidence in the Saints.
Verses 6-15	Paul's Concern as to Disorderly Behaviour.
Verses 16-18	Paul's Conclusion or Salutation.

The Day of the Lord and Vindication - Promotional

Chapter 1 begins and ends with God and the Lord Jesus Christ. It begins with grace and peace (v.2) and ends with grace and glory (v.12). After his usual salutation (vv.1-2), the apostle Paul records his thankfulness for the spiritual growth and steadfastness of the Thessalonian believers (vv.3-5). He then reveals to them the outcome of their persecution (vv.6-10) and finally makes known his remembrance of them in prayer (vv.11-12). Thus we can divide the chapter into four sections:- vv.1-2 The Introduction to the Epistle; vv.3-5 The Increase in the Saints - Paul never forgot an assembly of the saints and no man had a greater interest in the spread of the gospel or a greater concern for the assemblies; vv.6-10 The Intervention of God - all things are under the control of God who will one day intervene in His affairs; vv.11-12 The Intercession of Paul for the Saints.

Verses 1-2 The Introduction.
Verse 1. "Paul, and Silvanus, and Timotheus," Although the apostle Paul is undoubtedly the writer of the epistle he includes in his salutation his fellow-workers Silvanus (Silas) and Timotheus (Timothy) who were involved with him in the planting of the assembly at Thessalonica. They were also with him at Corinth when he wrote this epistle. Silas is mentioned first, being older than Timothy and joining the apostle in the work before Timothy. He was one of the "chief men among the brethren" (Acts 15.22) and a prophet (Acts 15.32). He, like Paul, was a Jew (Acts 16.20) and a Roman citizen (Acts 16. 37-38). Apart from the book of the Acts he is only mentioned in the opening salutations of the Thessalonian epistles and in

2 Corinthians 1.19. However, it is commonly accepted that Silvanus, a faithful brother, referred to in 1 Peter 5.12 is the same person. Timothy was a young man from Lystra (Acts 16.1; 1 Tim. 4.12), saved through the apostle Paul (1 Tim 1.2; 2 Tim 1.2) and "well reported of by the brethren at Lystra and Iconium." (Acts 16.2). He had a Jewish mother and a Gentile father (Acts 16.1). He is mentioned in all of Paul's epistles except Galatians, Ephesians and Titus. He is also mentioned in Hebrews 13.23 which many take as evidence that Paul was the writer of that epistle. Both Silas and Timothy joined the apostle on his second missionary journey (Acts 15.40; 16.3) and were among the first to bring the gospel to Europe (Acts 16.12). The mention of these fellow-workers indicates the harmony of these servants in their labours in Thessalonica. They were from different age groups with different backgrounds and different abilities, but harmoniously linked together in the work of God. They served the same Master and were one in purpose and interest, seeking to carry out the will of God. Every believer has been bought with the same price (1 Cor 6.20), should be subject to the same Lord, governed by the Word of God and should seek to carry out the will of God.

"unto the church of the Thessalonians" The epistle is addressed to the church of the Thessalonians. The Greek word translated 'church' is *ekklesia* and is formed from two Greek words *ek* which means 'out' and *kaleo* meaning 'to call'. Thus *ekklesia* means a company called out for a particular purpose and is better translated 'assembly' as in Acts 19.32, 39, 41. Here it refers to a company of believers called out to bear a collective testimony to all the truth of God, for the pleasure and glory of God. The form of address ' unto the church of the Thessalonians' is unique and brings before us the principle that believers in a locality should be gathered together in the Name of the Lord Jesus Christ in that locality. God intended that every believer should be a part of the assembly in the locality where they live thus maintaining a harmonious collective testimony for God in keeping with His word. This form of address indicates the composition of the assembly as well as its locality.

"in God our Father and the Lord Jesus Christ:" The expression "in God our Father and the Lord Jesus Christ" refers to the sphere of the assembly. The preposition 'in' governs both 'God our Father' and 'the Lord Jesus Christ' indicating the equality of the Father and the Son, thus emphasising the deity of the Lord Jesus Christ. The assembly was grounded, and existed, in the sphere and power of God our Father and the Lord Jesus Christ. 'In God our Father' indicates relationship. It shows that the assembly was separate from gentile idolatry and was a contrast to all paganism (the heathen temple). It also indicates that the assembly was in the tender care of the Father and was the object of His love. In 1 Thessalonians the apostle addressed the assembly as being 'in God the Father' indicating the fact of relationship, but here he uses the expression 'in God our Father' indicating fellowship in that relationship. 'In the Lord Jesus Christ would indicate redemption, it contrasts the assembly with what was Judaistic and shows that it was separate from the Jewish synagogue. It also indicates that the Lord Jesus Christ was not only the subject of its testimony, but also the source of power for that testimony which was subject to His lordship.

Verse 2. "Grace unto you," The salutation ends with the desire of Paul for them to have grace and peace. It has been stated that grace is the Greek form of greeting and peace the Hebrew form. Grace has brought salvation to us and salvation brings peace with God. Grace is the transforming power of God operating in our lives enabling us to live for God in every circumstance of life. It was this grace that was necessary for the Thessalonian believers to continue in their testimony for God in the face of the opposition and persecution they were enduring. It is this grace that is necessary for every believer to carry out the word of God whatever the circumstances.

"and peace," Peace is often looked on as the result of grace and often that is the case. However here both grace and peace come from God and thus peace here refers to inward tranquillity in spite of the circumstances in which they were found. Paul desired that they would be in a state of well being in the midst of the opposition and persecution they were experiencing. It is important that in the trials, difficulties and problems of life the believer rests in the Lord knowing He is still on the throne and remembers His own.

"from God our Father and the Lord Jesus Christ." In one sense grace and peace come both from God the Father and the Lord Jesus Christ, but they can be looked on as coming from God the Father (the source) and through the Lord Jesus Christ (the channel).

Verses 3-5   The Increase in the Saints.
In this section the apostle records his reasons for thanksgiving to God (v.3) in their endurance of persecution (v.4) which was an evidence that God was for them and against their persecutors (v.5).

Verse 3 The Thanksgiving of the Servants.
"We are bound to thank God always for you, brethren," The responsibility of the servants to offer thanksgiving to God is indicated in the expression 'we are bound to thank God'. The Greek word translated 'bound' (*opheilo*) means to owe as a debt or to be under an obligation to another. It expresses a sense of responsibility and is translated 'owe' in Romans 13.8, "owe no man anything, but to love one another:" and 'ought' in Ephesians 5.28, "So ought men to love their wives as their own bodies." It indicates a debt incurred which would be a dishonour not to pay. Here it refers to a special debt of gratitude for what grace had wrought in the Thessalonian believers which was a definite answer to the apostle's constant prayer for them (1 Thess 3.10-13). We have a responsibility, as the people of God, to offer constantly thanksgiving to God for all that He has bountifully bestowed upon us. The word translated 'thanks' has the thought of giving free and joyful gratitude to God. The word 'brethren' indicates the close relationship between the servants and the saints.

"as it is meet," The righteousness of the thanksgiving to God is indicated in this expression. The word 'bound' gives the subjective side of thanksgiving, i.e. what was due to God because of answered prayer, but the word 'meet' gives the objective side, i.e. the duty of the servants because of the saints' growth. The Greek word translated 'meet' (*axios*) has the thought of value, worth or weight and here indicates what is deserving. It is translated 'due reward' in Luke 23.41, "And we indeed justly; for we receive the due reward of our deeds:" and 'worthy' in The Revelation 5.2, "Who is worthy to open the book, and to loose the seals thereof?" God is worthy to receive thanksgiving from His people and it is only right that believers render to Him what is His due.

"because that your faith groweth exceedingly," The word 'because' introduces the reasons for the servants' thanksgiving, first in relation to their faith and then in relation to their love. The practical and energetic character of their faith, in spite of the persecution, is in view here. 'Groweth exceedingly' comes from one Greek word *huperauxano* which only occurs here and means to grow abundantly or beyond measure. It is a superlative and indicates that the growth of their faith was beyond the expectation of the apostle Paul, who had been anxious regarding them (1 Thess 3.1-5). Faith is the energetic principle of the Christian life which includes both personal confidence and absolute trust in God.

"and the charity of every one of you all toward each other aboundeth;" This rapid growth in faith was coupled with their love that abounded towards each other. The Greek word translated 'aboundeth' (*pleonazo*) means to overflow and is the very word, translated 'increase', used by the apostle Paul in his prayer for the Thessalonian saints (1 Thess 3.12), which had now been answered. Their love was overflowing like water irrigating the soil, i.e. having a beneficial affect upon others. Here we have the impartiality and abounding character of their love which Paul desired for them (1 Thess 4.9-10). That love was mutual, being both individual and corporate. Love permeated the assembly in Thessalonica testifying to the fact that the saints were followers of Christ (John 13.35) and were in the enjoyment of new life - "Seeing ye have purified your souls in obeying the truth through the Spirit unto unfeigned love of the brethren, see that ye love one another with a pure heart fervently:" (1 Peter 1.22). It seems that persecution results in believers being drawn closer together. However the desire of the Spirit of God for every assembly is that each believer be characterised by the kind of faith and love displayed by the Thessalonians.

Since the apostle had written his first epistle there had been and increase in their faith and love, but the apostle doesn't mention their hope. It seems that their hope had become dim because of the severe persecution and the teaching of some that the day of the Lord was upon them. Paul in this epistle seeks to revive and stimulate their hope.

Verse 4 The Trial of the Saints.
"So that we ourselves glory in you in the churches of God" In v.3 we have thanksgiving to God, here we have glorying in the saints. The expression "we ourselves" is an emphatic expression in the verse and it indicates that Paul and his fellow-labourers could not refrain from boasting. The word translated 'glory' (*kauchaomai*) means 'to boast' and although Paul was slow to boast of himself (2 Cor 12.1; Gal 6.14) he could not contain himself in regard to the Thessalonian saints. This boasting was not in the Thessalonians' achievements, but in what God had wrought in their lives. Paul mentions his boasting not to puff them up, but to encourage them in their present circumstances. The apostle's boasting was in the assemblies of God. He was holding them up as an example in order to encourage other assemblies (*cf.* 2 Cor 8.1-7). In the first epistle the apostle writes of them being an example in their confession and conduct, here they are an example in their continuance despite adverse circumstances. The expression "churches of God" indicates that the assemblies had their origin in God and that each local assembly belonged to God - "ye are God's husbandry, ye are God's building." (1 Cor 3.9). Each local assembly is in existence for the glory of God and has no right to act as it likes. The local assembly should be governed solely by the Word of God, should own the lordship of Christ and should be controlled by the gracious Spirit of God.

"for your patience and faith" The word translated 'patience' (*hupomone*) means standing fast. It implies the character of being unswerving in purpose and loyalty despite the greatest trials and suffering. They neither sought to avenge themselves nor did they draw back because the pathway involved suffering. It refers to steadfast constancy, being translated 'patient continuance' elsewhere (Romans 2.7), and indicates enduring under pressure.

It is not a passive endurance here, but an active one, i.e. bearing up and steering a right course in spite of the opposition and affliction they were enduring because of love and loyalty. This quality is most important in the midst of suffering and is seen in its perfection in Christ - "Who, when he was reviled, reviled not again; when he suffered, he threatened not;" (1 Pet 2.23). Identification with the Lord Jesus Christ in a world opposed to Him inevitably involves suffering - "Beloved, think it not strange concerning the fiery trial which is to try you, as though some strange thing happened unto you:" (1 Pet 4.12). We need strength from the Lord for such endurance (Col 1.11) which is only learned through trial (Rom 5.3; Jam 1.3) and which perfects our character (Jam 1.4). However, it seems that it is the same faith that is mentioned in v.3, but is now manifesting itself in persecution.

"in all your persecutions and tribulations that ye endure:" The word translated 'persecutions' (*diogmos*) has the idea of being pursued and indicates the hostile activities of those who oppose God, the people of God and the truth of God. We are reminded in 2 Timothy 3.12 that "all that will live godly in Christ Jesus shall suffer persecution." The word translated 'tribulations' (*thlipsis*) has the thought of the pressure of circumstances and refers to the afflictions of life. Here it refers to the result of persecution. Whereas 'persecutions' describe the hostile activity of others, the word 'tribulations' (afflictions) refers to the physical and mental suffering of those persecuted. The word 'endure' has the idea of bearing up under, or measuring up to, something. The thought here is of holding out against continual persecution and affliction. Through the grace of God we are able to bear up in every circumstance of life.

Verse 5 The Token of Righteous Judgment.
"Which is a manifold token of the righteous judgment of God,"
Although the words "Which is" are not in the original text they are necessary to complete the English statement and to connect the verses. It is generally accepted that the expression "a manifest token" refers to the 'patience and faith' of the Thessalonian saints, i.e. their enduring faith was evidence that God was for them and against their persecutors. The word translated 'a manifest token' (*endeigma*) only occurs here and means evidence, proof or to

point out something. Here it seems to indicate that their enduring faith was a proof of their new life and a guarantee of the vindication of God. What was taking place was an earnest of the righteous judgment of God pointing to their ultimate deliverance and the inevitable punishment of those opposed to them - "which is to them an evident token of perdition, but to you of salvation, and that of God." (Phil 1.28). Thus, a manifest token of the righteous judgment of God was seen in the saints being enabled by God to endure the persecutions. It is also seen in the long suffering of God towards the persecutors thus giving them opportunity either to repent or to fill up the cup of their iniquity.

"that ye may be counted worthy of the kingdom of God," This token of God's righteous judgment was in order to declare the Thessalonian believers worthy of the kingdom of God. As to the present their endurance was proof that their faith in Christ was genuine, in regard to the future the righteous judgment of God would count them worthy of the kingdom. The expression 'counted worthy' (*kataxioo*) is a judicial term. It does not indicate any merit in the saints, but means 'to reckon or declare worthy' - not worthy of entering into the kingdom, but rather counted worthy of being part of it. It is only righteous that those in whom the moral power of the kingdom is operating should be counted worthy of a place in its manifestation. Their attitude to the persecutions and afflictions was proof that they were true subjects of the kingdom. The expression 'kingdom of God' indicates that God rules in that kingdom and it refers to the sphere where His rule is acknowledged. The title 'kingdom of heaven or the heavens', which occurs only in Matthew (also *cf.* Dan 4.26), indicates the place from where God rules. Both titles refer to the same kingdom (*cf.* Matt 13.11 with Luke 8.10; Matt 19.14 with Mark 10.14; Matt 19.23-24). References to the kingdom of God seem either to view it as present (Acts 8.12) and inward (Rom 14.17) or as future in its manifestation when the Lord Jesus Christ will sit upon the throne of His glory (Matt 25.31). Here the reference is to that future manifestation of the kingdom at the second advent of Christ. Entrance into the kingdom of God is through the new birth (John 3.5; *cf.* Matt 18.3).

"for which ye also suffer:" This expression does not indicate that their suffering was necessary to merit the kingdom, but that it was on behalf of, or in the interests of, the kingdom - "and these all do contrary to the decrees of Caesar, saying that there is another king, one Jesus." (Acts 17.7). The word 'also' links their suffering with the suffering of the apostle Paul. They were loyal to the king in His rejection and will be associated with Him in the glory of the kingdom - "If we suffer, we shall also reign with him:" (2 Tim 2.12).

Verses 6-10 The Intervention of God.

This section shows that the character of God will inevitably bring about the reversal of conditions. It brings before us the righteous basis of God's judgment; the revelation of the Lord Jesus Christ; and the retribution inflicted upon the ungodly. It is intended to comfort and encourage the saints who were experiencing persecution.

Verse 6. "Seeing it is a righteous thing with God" The opening expression of this verse looks back to the mention of the righteous judgment of God in v.5. The word translated 'seeing' (*eiper*) has the idea of 'since' or 'if so be' (*cf.* Rom 8.9,17; 1 Cor 15.15; 1 Pet 2.3) emphasising the fact of God's righteous dealings with man. There is no question as to the outcome of the righteous judgment of God since the token of it has already been given (*cf.* Phil 1.28). The apostle here explains what is involved in that righteous judgment.

"to recompense tribulation to them that trouble you;" The righteous character of God makes it inevitable that there is a future judgment. In the estimation of God it is only righteous to recompense tribulation to the persecutors. The word translated 'recompense' (*antapodidomi*) is translated elsewhere 'repay' (Rom 12.19), 'render' (1 Thess 3.9) and means to give back as equivalent or in return for something (*cf.* Luke 14.14; Rom 11.35). Recompense is a necessary act of righteousness and, although this is not evident today, it will be demonstrated in a coming day. In the context this recompense is to both the persecuted and the persecutors. God is going to reverse things and those who have sown tribulation by troubling the saints will receive tribulation and those who rest in the promises of God and endure will receive rest. Since God will recompense it behoves believers not to take revenge themselves. The apostle deals first with the recompense of the persecutors indicating that to recompense them with tribulation is according to the law of retribution which would be fully displayed in the "revelation of the righteous judgment of God." (Rom 2.5). God's recompense is here called 'tribulations' (*cf.* v.4) which is only used elsewhere of retribution to the ungodly in Romans 2.9. It is used here to parallel what they brought upon those whom they persecuted - "whatsoever a man soweth, that shall he also reap." (Gal 6.7). It is closely related to the word translated 'trouble' (*thlibo*) which refers to the pressures the Thessalonians were experiencing because of the antagonism of the persecutors. Thus the parallelism is intended to be a comfort and encouragement to the saints. If saints suffer so much in this unrighteous world what must the suffering of the ungodly at the hands of the righteous Judge be like?

Verse 7. "And to you who are troubled rest with us," Paul now turns to the recompense of the saints which he expresses as 'rest' before he continues with his main theme of the judgment of the wicked. It is suggested that this opening expression is parenthetical within the main subject of retribution upon the persecutors. The word translated 'rest' (*anesis*) is opposite to the word translated 'tribulation' and means a loosening or slackening of strain or tension. It has the idea of relaxing a taut string. It is used negatively in 2 Corinthians 2.13 and 7.5 of Paul having no rest in his spirit until Titus comes with his report of the assembly at Corinth. The verb form is found in Acts 16.26 of the prisoners bands being 'loosed'. Thus the thought in the word is that of relief or release from every form bondage or stress. Here it indicates relief from the pressures of persecution, from affliction. The time of this recompense of rest is disputed. There are three suggestions:-

(i) A present rest. Taking the previous expression as a parenthesis and because of the closing words of that expression "with us", it is suggested that the apostle had a present rest in view. The

Thessalonians now knew that the whole programme was secure in the hands of God and so, in view of their suffering, Paul would have them rest in God. The apostle would have them share his rest in view of what was going to take place. However, the meaning of the word 'rest' here makes a present rest unlikely since it refers to relief from the suffering they were experiencing through persecution.

(ii) Rest at the rapture. Relief from persecution of the saints of this present dispensation commences when the Lord comes to the air. C.F.Hogg and W.E.Vine state in their commentary, "The time indicated is not that at which the saints will be relieved of persecution, but that at which their persecutors will be punished. The time of relief for the saints had been stated in the earlier letter, 4:15-17; here passing reference to a fact within the knowledge of the readers was all that was necessary." This would be in keeping with the meaning of 'rest' and with viewing the statement as being parenthetical. It is certainly true that the rapture will end persecution for all the saints of this day of grace.

(iii) Rest at the manifestation of Christ. It is also suggested that what is in view is the fullness or display of rest in contrast to the display of retribution meted out on the persecutors. T.W.Smith has stated in his commentary that, "The mention of rest at the Appearing is to illustrate that this event, with such awful consequences for their persecutors, has no terror for their victims whose portion then is rest." We must also bear in mind that the principle of recompense is also applicable to the period between the rapture and the revelation of Christ. The saints of that time will suffer dreadful persecution and at the Lord's appearing will experience joyful relief. This third view does not require the opening statement to be taken as a parentheses and we feel it is more in keeping with the context.

"when the Lord Jesus shall be revealed from heaven" The word translated 'revealed' (*apokalupsis*) means to uncover or unveil and is generally translated 'revelation' (1 Pet 1.13; Rev 1.1). Thus the expression is literally 'in the revelation of the Lord Jesus from heaven' and refers to the coming of the Lord to the earth in all His majesty and glory. It introduces the fact that retribution is part of that day when the righteous ways of God will be publically displayed (*cf.* Rom 2.5). The Thessalonian believers must have felt their weakness in the face of persecution, but in this coming day the Lord will display His power in angelic hosts.

"with his mighty angels," The word translated 'power' (*dunamis*) refers to the inherent power of the Lord. Thus the expression is rendered 'angels of His might or power' to indicate the fact that they are but instruments of His power. The idea is that they are those in whom the power of the Lord is made manifest. Through them the Lord exercises His power through them to display the righteous judgment of God inflicted upon the wicked.

Verse 8. "In flaming fire" This opening expression, has been taken by some with the preceding verse and by others with the following expression. When taken with v.7 it indicates the awesome manifestation of the Lord Himself. The idea is of being clothed in flaming fire expressing His holiness and His judgment of evil. It is the robe of His overwhelming majesty and glory. In the Old Testament manifestations of God were sometimes associated with fire (Exod 3.2; 19.18; Is 30.30; 66.15) and this seems to be the link here. When the expression is taken with the following statement 'taking vengeance' it indicates the instrument or dreadfulness of the judgment meted out to the wicked (Lev 10.2; Deut 32.22). Both interpretations are applicable and suit the context. Taking them both would convey the character of the Lord first and then the inevitable result in the judgment of evil.

"taking vengeance" The word translated 'vengeance' (*ekdikesis*) here refers to that which proceeds out of justice in total contrast to the revenge of men which proceeds from vindictiveness, self-gratification or mere emotion. There is no thought of 'getting even' with another, but the meting out of punishment which His righteous character demands. Vengeance is an act of justice. Here it is that full justice is displayed in the indignation of a holy God against the wickedness of men. Since vengeance belongs to God alone (Deut 32.35; Ps 94.1) the expression "taking vengeance" along with the expression "in flaming fire" emphasises the deity of the Lord Jesus Christ.

"on them that know not God, and that obey not the gospel of our Lord Jesus Christ:" The repetition of the definite participle in the original text indicates that two distinctive classes will be the recipients of such vengeance - "them that know not God, and them that obey not the gospel of our Lord Jesus Christ." The first class are those who are deliberately ignorant, who wilfully ignore or neglect the evidence that God is (Rom 1.28; 1 Thess 4.5). The second class are those who deliberately reject the message of the gospel, who refuse to submit to the command of God to repent (Acts 17.30).

Verse 9. "Who" This relative pronoun includes both classes in v.8 and qualifies as well as defines those who will experience what follows. It indicates the kind of persons exposed to judgment. The idea seems to be "who, with all like them, shall be punished."

"shall be punished" The word 'punished' is translated from two Greek words '*dike*' and '*tio*'. '*Tino*' or '*Tio*' only occurs here and means 'to pay a price, as a penalty'. '*Dike*' occurs four times and is translated elsewhere judgment (Acts 25.15) and vengeance (Acts 28.4; Jude 7). This combination denotes what is right and indicates the execution of a just sentence which brings to a climax the display of God's righteousness.

"with everlasting destruction" The word translated 'everlasting' (*aionios*), which is generally translated 'eternal', describes the final and unending penalty that justice demands. The word destruction (*olethros*) does not mean the destruction of being, but the destruction of welfare or well-being. It has the idea of ruin and misery, and indicates the loss of blessing, peace and joy. This is the vengeance referred to in v.8.

"from the presence of the Lord," The word translated 'presence' (*prosopon*) is generally translated 'face' and the preposition 'from' (*apo*) can either indicate the result, or the source, of the punishment. If viewed as the result, that is away from the face of the Lord, it would contrast with the believers' hope and joy of seeing His face. It would thus indicate eternal loss in contrast to the eternal gain of the believer. If viewed as the source, that is proceeding from the face of the Lord, it would indicate the dreadful vengeance of the Lord meted out upon the wicked - "The face of the Lord is against them that do evil, to cut off the remembrance of them from the earth." (Psalm 34.16). The second view seems to be more in keeping with the context, although both views are feasible.

"and from the glory of his power;" From the manifestation of the majestic glory and inherent power of the Lord Jesus. The language is similar to Isaiah 2.19, 21 "for (from) fear (the terror) of the Lord, and for (from) the glory of his majesty, when he ariseth to shake terribly the earth." Glory is the display of what He is essentially - His kingly majesty and splendour. Power is the might of the Lord which is not only displayed in judgment, but is the foundation of the believer's strength (Eph 6.10). Both glory and power are involved in the judgment of God. C.F.Hogg and W.E.Vine state, "The punishment here described is thus irrevocable banishment from the presence of the Lord and from the unapproachable light in which He dwells, 1 Tim. 6.16, into the "outer darkness," where , as He Himself said, "shall be the weeping and gnashing of teeth," Matt 25.30."

Verse 10. This verse unfolds the effect of the manifestation of Christ in relation to the saints. It reveals that the believers are those on whom and by whom the glorious perfection of Christ is exhibited. In contrast to the judgment in the previous verses the manifestation of Christ will be a display of His glory to the astonishment of the world.

"When he shall come" The reference here is to the revelation of Christ already referred to in v.7. The expression indicates that although this event is absolutely certain, the time of its fulfilment has not been revealed.

"to be glorified in his saints," To see the saints so exalted will cause all to acknowledge the glory and greatness of the One through whom they have been exalted. The glory they reflect is His glory - "I am glorified in them" (John 17.10). The word translated 'glorified' (*endoxadzo*) only occurs elsewhere in v.12 and means to appear glorious. It indicates the glory and blessedness conferred upon those who, having trusted Christ, have been despised by the world. This is the outcome of their faith and the fulfilment of the earnest expectation of creation - "the manifestation of the sons of God" (Rom 8.19). In v.7 the angels manifest His power, here the saints manifest His glory. In the saints we have the glory of His grace, but in the ungodly we have the glory of His power (vv.8-9).

"and to be admired in all them that believe" The designation 'saints' in the previous statement is in contrast to 'them that know not God' and the expression here 'them that believe' is in contrast to 'they that obey not' (v.8). However, unlike v.8 where there are two classes, only one class is in view here. The word 'saints' indicate what they are (set apart for, and to, God) and the expression 'them that believe' indicate how they became saints. The word translated 'admired' (*thaumazo*) means to marvel or to wonder and is generally translated accordingly (Luke 2.18; 4.22; John 4.27; 7.15). The expression indicates the wonder and amazement of the onlookers at what the love, grace and wisdom of God had wrought in poor, sinful and destitute sinners. The amazed world will wonder at the outcome of God's eternal plan and purpose in regard to mankind. The tense of the expression 'that believe' looks back to the time when the Thessalonians had "turned to God from idols" (1 Thess 1.9).

"(because our testimony among you was believed)" Having mentioned 'saints' and those who believe in general, the apostle now applies this to the Thessalonian believers themselves. This parenthesis is intended to be an encouragement to them in their adverse circumstances and to assure them of a glorious future. The ultimate outcome of their faith would be Christ glorified and admired in them - "For I reckon that the sufferings of this present time are not worthy to be compared with the glory which shall be revealed in us." (Rom 8.18). What a glorious future for every child of God. Paul and his fellow-labourers had not only proclaimed the gospel to them, but had borne witness, by their lives, to the truth and power of that gospel in their lives.

"in that day." This is the day of the revelation of the Lord Jesus mentioned in v.7 which embraces the events of vv.6-10. It is called 'that day' because it is a great day when the greatness, grandeur and glory of the Lord Jesus will be manifested, when the saints will appear with Him in glory and when the wicked will be punished. It will be the time when earth's rightful King will come in all the majesty of His Person to set up His kingdom and to hold to account all who filled the earth with lawlessness, persecuted His people and rebelled against Him.

Verses 11-12 The Intercession of Paul

As in the first epistle the apostle mentions here his prayers on their behalf assuring them that he has not forgotten them. His prayer here is in relation to the subject of the passage, the coming Kingdom.

Verse 11. "Wherefore" This word not only introduces the intercession of Paul, but also takes us back to v.5 and continues the subject of the Thessalonians' being reckoned worthy of the kingdom, after the long parentheses of vv. 6-10. The word has the thought of 'to which end' indicating the purpose of the apostle's constant prayer.

"Also we pray always for you," The position of the word 'also' comes between the words 'we' and 'pray' making the word 'pray' emphatic as the subject of the passage. Paul had acknowledged their patience and faith in the midst of persecution (v.4) and that they suffered for the kingdom (v.5), and now, to encourage them, he assures them of his constant intercession for them that they may continue in that patience and faith. The example of Paul's constant intercession for the saints (*cf.* Phil 1.4; Col 1.9) is a challenge to us today in regard to our prayer life. The assurance of his prayers also indicated to them that the strength to enable them to continue came from God who was able to keep them from falling, and to present them faultless before the presence of his glory with exceeding joy, (Jude 24). The people of God in every generation and every circumstance of life are dependant upon God for the strength to live for Him (Phil 2.13) and thus the exhortation, "be strong in the grace that is in Christ Jesus." (2 Tim 2.1). The apostle Paul could write, "I can do all things through Christ which strengtheneth me" or as one has translated it "through Christ who continues to pour His strength into me." (Phil 4.13).

"that our God would count you worthy of his calling," Here we have the subject of the apostle's intercession which is in keeping with the mind of God. It is not that God would account them worthy in themselves, but, as v.5 states, He would reckon them worthy, i.e. reckon them worthy because their lives were in keeping with His calling. The calling here seems to be related to the future manifestation of the kingdom of God - "unto his kingdom and glory." (1 Thess 2.12). The thought here is that the saints, through the grace of God, demonstrate by their lives the power and glory of that kingdom. Believers today are responsible to live in view of that coming day and to allow the gracious Spirit of God to develop increasingly in their lives the features seen in all their perfection in the King.

"and fulfil" The word translated 'fulfil', (*pleroo*) means, in this context, to perform fully or to completion the work of grace. The tense indicates that the end result is in view. It has the idea of God, by His power, enabling the Thessalonian saints to manifest in their lives the purpose of their calling - "that ye would walk worthy of the vocation wherewith ye are called." (Eph 4.1). Our manner of life should be suitable to the calling and in keeping with the claims and character of the One who has called us.

"all the good pleasure of his goodness," Every good pleasure of goodness. The word translated "good pleasure" (*eudokia*) means 'good desire' and has the thought of a free and willing purpose. The word translated 'goodness' (*agathosune*) is only found elsewhere in Romans 15.14, Galatians 5.22 and Ephesians 5.9, and always refers to the quality of goodness in believers, which is the fruit of the Spirit. The whole phrase may be 'desire characterised by goodness' or 'desire after goodness'. It seems more likely to be desires which spring out of what God has wrought in them, i.e. every desire coming from regenerate minds being manifested in goodness.

"and the work of faith" Here we have the course and conduct of the Christian life which springs from faith. Actions that have their roots in God. Every activity of the Christian should be in keeping with the word of God and be for His pleasure and glory.

"with power" Although this can refer to the previous expression and the Thessalonian saints themselves, it is clear that every believer is completely dependant upon God for the energy to live for Him. It is God who produces spiritual desire in the Christian and gives the power to carry out that desire (Phil 2.13).

Verse 12. In verse 11 we have the contents of the apostle's prayer, now, in this verse, we have the purpose of his prayer.

"That the name of our Lord Jesus Christ may be glorified in you," In a coming day the Lord Jesus Christ will be glorified in the saints (v.10), but here Paul prays that even now His name might be glorified in the lives of the Thessalonian saints. The Christian life is not a set of rules or regulations, but a Person, even our Lord Jesus Christ - "Christ who is our life" (Col 3.4). He should fill our vision, occupy our minds, completely satisfy our hearts, captivate our wills, direct our footsteps and control our lives. The Christian life is Christ centred and only the enjoyment of Him will enable us to be what God intends us to be and thus, in our lives now, glorify the name of the Lord Jesus Christ. Spiritual fullness is found in Him and He is all sufficient to meet every need of the believer (Col 2.10). The increasing appreciation of our ascended and glorious Lord is the power which enables us to live for His glory and for the pleasure of God. Even in the midst of persecution the Thessalonian believers could, through spiritual desires and works of faith, glorify the name of the Lord Jesus Christ.

"and ye in him," The apostle, having mentioned the Lord being glorified in the saints, immediately thinks of a future day when the saints would be glorified in Christ. This glory of the saints is linked with their vital union with Christ and is mentioned in the Lord's prayer (John 17.22). We shall appear with Him in glory at His manifestation (Col 3.4), but in that event the emphasis is upon the Lord's glory. It seems that Paul now, having mentioned the Lord being glorified in the saints in a coming day and in their lives now, turns to the saints being glorified in Christ which will take place at the rapture. Then the saints will be morally and physically like Him since the resurrection and the change will have take place - "It is sown in dishonour; it is raised in glory:" (1 Cor 15.43) - He shall change the body of humiliation and fashion it like unto the body of His glory (Phil 3.21). That will be the moment when the saints will be glorified in Him - "when he shall appear, we shall be like him; for we shall see him as he is." (1 John 3.2).

"according to the grace of our God and the Lord Jesus Christ." This statement is to be taken with each phrase of the apostle's prayer - with the saints being reckoned worthy of their calling, with the fulfilling or the enabling of God for them to live for His glory (2 Cor 9.8; Tit 2.11-14) and with them being glorified in Him. It is grace from first to last - from the calling to the glorifying. We are nothing in ourselves and can do nothing in ourselves. We are completely dependant upon the Lord. We are undeserving of the least of His mercies (Gen 32.10) and at best we are unprofitable servants (Luke 17.10). We are what we are by the grace of God and all that we will be is because of His grace (1 Cor 15.10). It has been pointed out that there is only one article in the expression "our God and the Lord Jesus Christ" and thus it reads literally 'our God and Lord Jesus Christ' implying only one Person. Here it is not the thought of oneness of divine Persons, but rather of grace in and through the Person of the Lord Jesus Christ which accomplishes divine purpose.

The Day of the Lord and Explanation - Prophetical.

In ch.1 the apostle seeks to comfort and encourage the saints in the midst of their severe persecution, whereas in ch.2 he seeks to caution and enlighten them as to the day of the Lord. In ch.1 he sets them at rest with regard to outward persecution, but now in ch.2 he seeks to bring inward tranquillity to their disturbed minds. When circumstances come about that we neither expect or anticipate and which are difficult to explain we are often tempted to misunderstand them. This is exactly what had taken place at Thessalonica. The Thessalonian believers evidently knew that there was going to be a time of suffering, called the great tribulation (Matt 24.21), and that the day of the Lord would bring great trials and affliction upon the world. Because of the circumstances they were passing through and because of false teaching, they assumed that they were already in the day of the Lord. Paul shows this was not the case for they, as believers, were exempt from that time of suffering which was to come upon the earth. They actually belonged to a different programme and thus from v.13 there is a complete change of subject. Instead of God's dealing with the world and the man of sin we now have His dealings with His people which is in sharp contrast to the previous subject. Thus vv.1-12 show that the believers of this present day of grace are not involved in the day of the Lord and vv.13-17 show that God has another programme for them and that all was in order as far as they were concerned.

Verses 1-12 Concerning the Day of the Lord.

This section is one of the most difficult passages in the New Testament. The saints of Thessalonica had been grounded in the truth of the Lord's coming and this was their blessed hope as is evident from 1 Thess 1.10. It so occupied them that the death of some of the saints caused them deep anxiety. The apostle alleviated this anxiety in his first epistle (4.13-18). They should have known from that first letter that the day of the Lord would not overtake them and that they would not endure the wrath of that coming day (5.1-11). However it is clear that, through the false teaching of the Judaistic element, they had become confused concerning the sequence of events. This confusion arose from the fact that the false teachers established, from the Old Testament scriptures, that the Lord's coming was a day of darkness, suffering and judgment. They used the present affliction and persecution to convince the Thessalonian believers that the day of the Lord had come. In this section Paul exposes the error of such teaching in order to dispel their confusion and fear, and to revive their hope. In vv.1-4 the apostle beseeches the saints and then in vv.5-12 he reminds them of his oral teaching when he was with them.

Verses 1-4 Paul Beseeches the Saints.
In the opening verses Paul deals with the disturbed condition of the minds of the saints and why that condition had come about. He then unfolds the reasons why the day of the Lord could not be present. He sets out the prophetic events in chronological order - the rapture, the apostasy, the manifestation of the man of sin and then the day of the Lord. It is important to note that Paul first establishes the truth of the rapture before dealing with the false teaching concerning the day of the Lord.

Verse 1. "Now we beseech you, brethren," The word 'Now' links the closing verses of ch.1 with the opening statements of this chapter. It seems evident that the apostle, in his appeal here, continues the sublime thought of the saints being glorified in Christ at His coming. The word translated 'beseech' means to ask or request. Paul is not commanding them as an apostle but affectionately beseeching them as a brother. He treats them as brethren who possess the same life and are in the same family. The word 'brethren' not only indicates spiritual relationship, but conveys the thought of endearment and warmth. The apostle used the term 18 times in his first epistle to them and 6 times in this letter. Paul used it in all his epistles thus manifesting his love for all the saints. "Brethren" is not a denominational name but a term that applies to every believer - "he is not ashamed to call them brethren." (Heb 2.11). Sad to say this term is used in an unscriptural way today implying that assemblies are a denomination, which is not true. To say one belongs to the brethren meaning one meets with believers gathered to the Lord's name is not only unscriptural but also misleading.

"by the coming of our Lord Jesus Christ," There is a difference of opinion as to the meaning of the Greek word *huper* translated 'by' in this context, whether Paul is beseeching 'by' or 'touching' the coming of our Lord. The first is the correct rendering since if the second was accepted the first two verses would imply that the coming of the Lord and the day of the Lord are the same event. Then the apostle would be beseeching the saints using the very subject that perplexed them. This cannot be contemplated and is contrary to the purpose of Paul which was to alleviate the anxiety of the saints. He is turning their minds to what he had written in his first epistle concerning the Lord's coming. Thus he uses the same Greek word *parousia* (translated coming) meaning presence - His presence with His own instead of His absence. His purpose is to remove their confusion by establishing them in the truth of the rapture and thus restoring to them their blessed hope. This blessed hope would not only cheer them, but would also confirm that they would not be involved in the day of the Lord. He is saying, get your minds off the day of the Lord and riveted upon the Lord's coming. Don't go by your emotions but by the truth of God. At the coming of the Lord they would be taken away before that day of wrath (1 Thess 1.10).

"and (by) our gathering together unto him," It is necessary to point out that this second 'by' is not in the original text and that its insertion implies two events instead of the one event, the rapture. Both statements clearly refer to the rapture of the saints in this day of grace to meet the Lord in the air and to be with Him forever. This expression briefly summarises the teaching of 1 Thess 4.15-17 of which the saints at Thessalonica would be reminded.

The Greek word translated 'gathering together' (*episunagorge*) is only found elsewhere in Heb 10.25 where it is translated 'assembling together' - "Not forsaking the *assembling* of ourselves *together*,". There Christ is the gathering centre of companies of believers here on earth. They are gathered together unto His name outside the camp bearing His reproach (Matt 18.20; Heb 13.13). Such gatherings look forward to that glorious meeting with Him in the air and are a foretaste of that great gathering to Him. Our gathering together unto Him in that coming day will terminate the gatherings unto Him here.

Verse 2. "that ye be not soon shaken in mind, or troubled," This is the aim of the apostle's appeal and indicates that a right understanding of the rapture would steady their thinking. The idea here is of a sudden shock which takes one by surprise and startles. The saints had been shaken in their understanding of events. This had left them in a troubled and agitated state of mind. "In mind" refers to the controlling faculty of reason, understanding and judgment. Paul was saying 'do not allow anything to disturb correct understanding of the subject' or 'do not be knocked off balance in the truth of God.' Nothing should move the believer from the truth of God. In ch.1.7 they were troubled by persecution from without, but here they are troubled from within, in their minds. The one often leads to the other. In ch.1 the result of the persecution was that they were standing fast, but here because of misunderstanding and false teaching there was a danger of them being shaken from their moorings and being emotionally disturbed. Sometimes what we fear most is not the most dangerous. Outward persecution may not be the most perilous, but it could lead to distress of mind which is far more painful. Although we can see the physical sufferings of fellow believers we cannot enter into the sufferings of the mind. We do not know what upset of mind and mental turmoil some dear saints might be passing through. Often it is difficult to know how to sympathise with them. We can link these two things with the twofold character of the devil. In the persecution of 1.7 he is seen as a roaring lion (1 Pet 5.8), here, in the false teaching, he is seen as an angel of light (2 Cor 11.14). Satan cannot destroy us, but he can distress us. If he cannot do it outwardly he will seek to do it inwardly and sometimes he will do both at the same time as seen here.

"neither by spirit," This suggests a professed prophetic utterance which implies a message brought by some who claimed the gift of prophecy. We must remember that this gift was still then in operation (1 Cor 12.28; 1 Thess 5.20). However, it is always necessary to "try the spirits whether they are of God:" (1 John 4,1). When any teaching is contrary to the Word of God it is coming from false teachers who are generally influenced by an evil spirit. We must be careful to place teaching alongside the truth of God.

"nor by word," This error was being publically taught either as the result of human logic and reasoning or alleging it had come from the apostle Paul. It seems that the oral teaching of the Judaisers is in view, the kind of teaching that has its source in human speculation and supposition. We are reminded that human reasoning and speculation is opposite to faith and that "the natural man receiveth not the things of the Spirit of God: .... neither can he know them, because they are spiritually discerned." (1 Cor 2.14).

"nor by letter as from us," This clearly refers to a letter forged in Paul's name, written to affirm that they were in the day of the Lord. In this threefold way the enemy sought to deceive and distress the saints and to dislodge them from the solid rock of divine truth concerning the rapture. The devil will always seek to turn believers away from the truth and will use any means to do so - "let us, who are of the day, be sober, putting on the breastplate of faith and love; and for an helmet, the hope of salvation." (1 Thess 5.8).

"as that the day of Christ is at hand." It is generally accepted that the expression "the day of Christ" should be "the day of the Lord". The context would support this since the day in view cannot begin until the falling away and the manifestation of the man of sin (v.3). However, the day of Christ commences at the rapture before these events, and it refers to the events during the Lord's presence with His own (the Church) between the rapture and the revelation of the Lord Jesus Christ. Whereas the day of Christ has to do with events in heaven, the day of the Lord has to do with events on earth. The former has to do with the Church and includes the Judgment Seat of Christ and the marriage of the Lamb and ends with the manifestation of Christ (v.8). The day of the Lord includes the great tribulation (Matt 24.21-19), the manifestation of Christ (Zech 14.1-3; Rev 19.11-21), the restoration of Israel (Is 14.1-4; Ezek 37.12-14; Amos 9.11-15), all the events of the Millennium when Christ will be in the midst of Israel (Zeph 3.11-17) and ends with the desolation of the heavens and the earth (2 Pet 3.10). It is different to the day of God (2 Pet 3.12) which refers to the new heavens and the new earth where righteousness will dwell, the eternal state. In the day of the Lord He will assert His authority in contrast to today, man's day, when man seeks to dominate and control things. The Greek word translated "at hand" is generally translated 'present' (*cf.* Rom 8.38; 1 Cor 7.26) thus the false inference was that the day of the Lord was present.

Verse 3. "Let no man deceive you by any means:" This looks back to the three things in the previous verse, but also implies that other means of deceit could be used to deceive them. The word translated 'deceive' (*exapatao*) is used elsewhere:- of sin deceiving (Rom 7.11), of men deceiving (Rom 16.18), of self deception (1 Cor 3.18) and of Satan beguiling Eve (2 Cor 11.3). Paul is emphasising that, whatever means were used to prove that the day of the Lord was present, it was not so. They should not have allowed anything to disturb their minds. They should not have been shaken out of their peaceful mind and left in a troubled state. This warning exhortation implies that their troubled state of mind was needless.

"for that day shall not come," That day was not present and Paul is going to give the reason why it hadn't come. There are certain events which must take place before the day of the Lord commences. The apostle is seeking to comfort the saints by indicating that there is a period of time between the rapture and the commencement of that coming day. Believers today should not be marked by consternation because of events in the world as we know that no prophetic event can take place before the coming of the Lord for His own. God's prophetic clock has stopped and will not start again until after the rapture. Although a number of events will take place after the rapture and before the commencement of the day of the Lord, Paul only mentions two, the falling away and the revealing of the man of sin.

"except there come a falling away first," This emphasises the fact that the day of the Lord could not be present. The Greek word translated 'falling away' (*apostasia*) means apostasy, an abandoning of God and His word. There is a definite article here, 'the apostasy', indicating a general and world wide falling away. The principles of apostasy have been, and are, at work, but this is the full development of it which will take place after the Lord's coming for His own. Apostasy is a deliberate action of turning away from the things of God to falsehood. It is seen throughout the Old Testament and Paul writes to Timothy about it, "some shall depart from the faith" (1 Tim 4.1; *cf.* 2 Tim 3; 2 Pet 3; Jude). Apostasy involves transferring one's professed allegiance from God to another. We must point out that apostasy cannot characterise a true believer or a heathen. There cannot be apostasy without some kind of profession regarding divine revelation. It always implies unreality, a professed belief which is completely set aside. The apostasy indicates a universal abandonment, by the masses, of what they profess to believe and a total turning of their backs on God and His word. It will be a wholesome repudiation of God and His word by professed Christianity and by Judaism. Both Jews and Gentiles will be involved in the apostasy. It will be a turning away from God to a false god. The action of these Thessalonian believers was opposite to this as they had turned to God from idols (1 Thess 1.9).

"and the man of sin be revealed," The apostasy will be the ground from which the man of sin will spring. The expression "the man of sin" refers to an individual. It is not a system, and it indicates the character of the man, implying that sin has complete dominion over him. His will willingly submits to sin's dictates. There is a difference of opinion as to the identity of this person among many spiritual and able teachers. Many commentators consider that he is the second beast of Rev 13 while others think he is the first. However, although one must come to one's own conclusion, this is not a subject for friction, but for forbearance. We believe prophetic scripture points to the first beast as being the man of sin, the antichrist (1 Jn 2.18), the little horn (Dan 7 & 8), the coming prince (Dan 9) and the wilful king (Dan 11.36). He is not only opposed to Christ and all that is of God, but he is also a counterfeit of Christ. He is the man of sin in contrast to Christ, the Man of holiness. The word translated 'revealed' (*apokalupta*) means to unveil or to manifest and is used in ch 1.7. It is used again of this event in vv.6 & 8. This is not his rise, which takes place before Daniel's 70th week (Dan 9.24-27), but his manifestation which will take place in the midst of that week when he is given the kingdom (Rev 17.17). The 7 year period of Daniel's 70th week doesn't commence until the signing of the covenant by the beast and the mass of apostate Jews (Dan 9.27). Thus he will be in prominence before the beginning of the 7 year period and in existence long before that. Prior to his being revealed as the man of sin he is a deceiver, winning the confidence of the majority. His true character will not be seen until his revelation when the covenant is broken (Dan 9.27). There are two great unveilings that this world will witness in this epistle. In chapter 1 we have the glorious manifestation of Christ in all His majesty and might. In this chapter we have the revelation of the man of sin which puts his claim beyond question in the eyes of the world in general. Then his hostility to God and His people, as well as his self-exaltation, will be revealed. The first half of Daniel's 70th week (31/2 years) will see the full development of the apostasy. The second half is the duration of his supremacy (Dan 7.25; Rev 13.5).

"the son of perdition:" This expression is only used elsewhere of Judas (John 17.12) and refers to the destiny of a person - "he went to his own place (Acts 1.25). The word translated 'perdition' (*apoleia*) means perish. It always carries with it the idea of disaster and here it refers to the end of the man of sin and his doom. It is not without significance that the first time this man is mentioned his character is given, followed immediately by his doom which is the consequence of what he is. All his plans to displace God and His word will come to nought and he will perish. Since he will exalt himself in impiety, so he will be cast down to eternal punishment.

Verse 4 This verse reveals the preeminence of this man's sin which justifies the title 'the man of sin'. We note his four actions - he opposes, he exalts himself, he sits and he shows himself.

"Who opposes and exalteth himself above all that is called God," He opposes and exalts himself not only above the true God, but also above idols and any kind of religion. He will oppose God not only in action but also in speech - "he shall speak great words against the most High," (Dan 7.25) - ""shall speak marvellous things against the God of gods," (Dan 11.36) - "And he opened his mouth in blasphemy against God," (Rev 13.6). He will be a brilliant orator with ability to sway the masses. He will use his powerful oratory to blaspheme the name of God. Bitterly opposed to God and the things of God, he will take every opportunity to speak against God and further his own ends in seeking to elevate himself above God. His flowing speech will captivate the multitudes, drawing them to himself and binding them together in an atheistic unity. What a contrast to the gracious words which proceeded out of the Lord's mouth (Luke 4.22). "He shall exalt himself, and magnify himself above every god," (Dan 11.36). He will be full of pride and consider he is the greatest and so will devise plans to glorify himself. What a contrast to our blessed Lord who humbled Himself (Phil 2.8) and who alone could truthfully say "I am meek and lowly of heart" (Matt 11.29). We need to challenge ourselves by asking, "are we like our blessed Lord or are we characterised by pride?". In his arrogance the man of sin will do his own will having his own ends before him in contrast to the Lord Jesus Christ who came not to do His own will, but His Father's will (John 6.38).

"or that is worshipped;" He will not tolerate any object of worship except himself and his master, Satan. Thus at his revelation, in the midst of the week, the harlot of Revelation 17 will be destroyed (*cf*. Rev 17.16-17) and the sacrifices of Israel will be swept away (Dan 8.11; 9.27; 11.31). He will make sure that there will be no religion whatsoever and no object of adoration and worship except the dragon and himself (Rev 13.4).

"so that he as God sitteth in the temple of God," This will be a definite moment when he will take his seat in the temple and make his claim to be God. He will claim that his entrance into the temple is the fulfilment of Malachi 3.1 "the Lord, whom ye seek, shall suddenly come to his temple,". The words "as God" has not the thought of 'as God sits there', for He is not there, but 'as if he was God'. It is not that he will claim to be Jehovah, but rather that he, and not Jehovah, is God. The word translated 'temple' (*naos*) means the inner shrine, the dwelling place of God, and the added words "of God" means that the reference could not be to a heathen temple. The definite article infers an actual structure and thus the reference is to the temple that will be rebuilt in Jerusalem. The arrogance and pride of the man of sin will rise to its pinnacle in this impious act of rebellion against God. He contemptuously takes his seat in the temple demanding veneration from all. Those who believe the man of sin is the second beast of Revelation 13 take this expression as indicating Jerusalem is his centre, and he is the religious head in contrast to the first beast who is the political head of the ten kingdom confederacy. However, both offices were seen in Nebuchadnezzar and in the Roman Emperors and are seen today in the Pope, and in the Queen who is head of state and head of the church of England. More significant is that both kingship and priesthood are combined in the Lord Jesus Christ - "he shall be a priest upon his throne:" (Zech 6.13). Just as Christ is King Priest so the antichrist, the man of sin, Satan's counterfeit, will combine both offices in himself. As the Lord Jesus receives worship and through Him the Father is worshipped, even so the man of sin will be worshipped and through him the dragon will be worshipped (Rev 13.4, 8). An image, it seems of the antichrist and called the abomination of desolation (Dan 9.27; 11.31; 12.11; Matt 24.15; Rev 13.14-15), will be erected on the temple that he and the dragon might be worshipped through it. The devil has always sought worship (Matt 4.9). There is no scripture to suggest that the second beast of Revelation 13 is worshipped. Satan and the two beasts of Revelation 13 form the trinity of evil in contrast to the Holy Trinity, with Satan as the counterfeit of the Father, the first beast the counterfeit of Christ and the second beast the counterfeit of the Spirit.

"shewing himself that he is God." Giving a display to show he is in the place that belongs to God. One great design will be in his mind and that will be to take the position that God alone deserves. Being satanically driven he will seek to rob God of His glory seeking supremacy for himself and Satan (Isa 14.12-14). He will not be hid, but will present himself to the world. He will appeal to the Jew and the Gentile and claim to be able to solve the international problems of the world. He will be despotic, the devil's puppet, holding universal sway. His rule will be world wide and he will have his throne in the rebuilt city of Babylon, as well as his seat in Jerusalem. He will emphasise and express humanitarianism - the devil's lie, "ye shall be as gods," (Gen 3.5). The world today is being prepared for this coming man - politically, commercially, socially and religiously.

Verses 5-12 Paul Reminds the Saints.
The apostle reminds the saints of his past teaching. The problems we see in these verses would never have arisen if we knew all that Paul had taught the Thessalonian saints on this subject. These believers were not in the day of the Lord because there was, and is, a restraint and a restrainer holding back the evil designs of the devil. Thus that day could not have come as they thought it had. However the evil principle of lawlessness, which reaches its climax in the man of sin, is already at work. Having mentioned the revelation of the man of sin, the apostle immediately refers to his destruction at the glorious manifestation of Christ. Paul throws further light on the character of this man by stating that his power will be satanic and that miracles accompany his manifestation. Those who love unrighteousness and turn their back on the truth will be deceived by these signs. God will take judicial dealings with such by sending them a strong delusion so that they will become followers of the Lawless One thinking that they have the truth. The result will be their eternal damnation.

Verse 5. "Remember ye not, that, when I was yet with you, I told you these things?" This is a kindly reproof. They would not have been disturbed in mind if they only had remembered his teaching. It was not that they didn't accepted what he taught them, but they had been shaken by false teaching. It is amazing that although Paul's was not long in Thessalonica he took time to instruct the saints in prophetic matters. It is evident from this that young believers do have the capacity to receive such truths. The gracious Spirit of God, who indwells the child of God, not only gives the believer an interest in the truth, but also the ability to take it in. He wrote this epistle to confirm what he had taught when he was with them. The teaching of the apostle hadn't changed no matter what others were teaching. Their endurance in the midst of persecution, their growth in faith and their love, were all evident because they had received the truth from the apostle. How important it is to pass on the truth of God to the on coming generation - "the things that thou hast heard of me among many witnesses, the same commit thou to faithful men, who shall be able to teach others also." (2 Tim 2.2). The older generation of believers are responsible to convey the truth of the Word of God to a younger generation. It may be that the worldliness and materialism prevalent among Christians today is because there has been, and still is, failure in passing on all the truth of God. In may appear that there are some obscure portions in this chapter. This is because Paul had already taught these prophetic truths to the Thessalonian saints while he was with them.

Verse 6. "And now ye know what withholdeth" This statement indicates that the Thessalonian saints, through Paul's oral ministry, knew full well what was preventing the full force of lawlessness and the revealing of the man of sin. The word translated 'withholdeth' (*katecho*) means 'to hold fast or back' (1 Thess 5.21; Luke 4.42) and is translated 'letteth' in the following verse. In both verses the word has the idea of restraining, albeit with this important difference, that in this verse it is in the neuter gender, but in v.7 it is in the masculine gender. Thus in this verse it is the element or principle which is the restraint, whereas in v.7 it is a person who restrains. There is a difference of opinion as to what the restraint is in this verse. Some have suggested the Roman Empire, others the powers that be, since they are ordained of God (Rom 13.1-7). However, most commentators suggest that the Church or body of believers upon earth during this day of grace is the restraint. In support of this it is stated that the body of believers on earth are "the salt of the earth:" (Matt 5.13) and is preventing the advancement of corruption and lawlessness. It is also stated that the indwelling Holy Spirit is the strength of the body of believers on earth holding back the wave of unrighteousness. Thus while the Church period runs its course the man of sin cannot be revealed. Although this statement is true it does not necessarily justify the conclusion that the Church or body of believers on earth is the restraint referred to in this verse. We must remember that the statement "Ye are the salt of the earth:" is not only applicable to the saints of this day of grace, but also to the saints in the period between the rapture and the revelation of Christ. Thus the statement does not really support the suggestion. Since the purpose of the restraint is to prevent the revealing of the man of sin until the time determined by God we believe the power of the Spirit of God is the restraint in this verse. Only the power of God can hold back the plans of Satan.

"that he might be revealed in his time." This statement gives the purpose of the restraint - to the end that the man of sin, in whom will be seen the fullness of lawlessness, may be revealed in his time. The word translated 'time' (*kairos*) signifies a definite or fixed period, but it refers to the characteristics rather than the length or date of that period. It is translated 'seasons' in 1 Thessalonians 5.1 alongside the Greek word '*chronos*' which refers to the duration of a period. The man of sin cannot be revealed until the day is morally suitable for his presence. Thus it is not until the apostasy is in its fullness that he will be revealed as that is the fertile ground from which he will spring up. It is evident that the time and duration of his season is determined by God and that the restraint will continue until God's appointed time. God has His own purposes of grace and prophetic fulfilment and Satan cannot bring in his programme, which will be short and which will end in destruction, until allowed of God.

Verse 7. "For the mystery of iniquity doth already work:" The word 'for' introduces the purpose for the restraint mentioned in the previous verse and also indicates the reason why the saints were suffering affliction. The word translated 'mystery' (*musterion*) does not mean what is mystical or mysterious, but that which is kept secret by God and can only be known by divine revelation. These secrets are only made known in God's appointed time (Col 1.26). Their significance is that they are truths revealed by God including the revelation of Himself in Christ (Job 11.7; Col 2.2). It is only believers who can perceive what is revealed by God since the unregenerate cannot receive these truths because they are spiritually discerned (1 Cor 2.14). There are a number of these mysteries in the New Testament beginning with the 'mysteries of the kingdom of heaven' (Matt 13.11) and concluding with the 'Mystery, Babylon the Great' (Rev 17.5-7). Here in this verse we have the 'mystery of iniquity'. The word translated 'iniquity' (*anomia*) means lawlessness, the setting aside of law and all restraints. The thought here is the overthrowing of divine government and principles. It is the deliberate defiance of the word and claims of God in contrast to the mystery of godliness (1 Tim 3.16). The principle or spirit of lawlessness is already at work. It is not only operative in the world and in Christendom, but also in many assemblies where the word of God is violated and the principles of gathering are set aside. The working out of this principle is referred to by the Lord in the parable of the leaven (Matt 13.33; Luke 13.20-21). It is also seen in Acts 20.30 "Also of your own selves shall men arise, speaking perverse things, to draw away disciples after them.", in 2 Tim 4.3-4 "For the time will come when they will not endure sound doctrine ..... And they shall turn away their ears from the truth, and shall be turned unto fables." and in Diotrephes who loved to have the preeminence (2 John 9). It was also at work in the assembly in Thessalonica (1 Thess 5.4; 2 Thess 3.6, 11-12). The spirit of lawlessness which is working today will become full blown in a coming day when all its features will be manifested in the man of sin. The working of lawlessness is the deification of man and is seen in humanism today. The devil has been working to this end (*cf.* Gen 3.5) in order to displace God. He has one end in view, the exalting of man and the worship of himself. The man of sin will seek to achieve this by overthrowing all that is of God and by making his own law. He will "cast down the truth to the ground:" (Dan 8.12) and "change times and laws:" (Dan7.25) and establish his own rule.. He will seek to stamp out all that is of God and introduce something completely different. It could be that he will change the Calendar that bears testimony to the first advent of Christ. He will introduce laws which will popularise sin and lusts of every kind. There may also be a reference to abolishing marriage and the setting aside of family relationships instituted by God at the beginning. He will do his own will (Dan 11.36) in contrast to the Lord Jesus Christ who came not to do His own will but the will of the Father who sent Him (John 3.30; 6.38).

"only he that now letteth will let," As mentioned in v.6 the word translated 'letteth' and 'let' (*katecho*) is the same as that translated 'withholdeth' there and has the thought of restraining. Here we have a person who restrains. W.E.Vine states, "in v.6 a principle is referred to, here that principle is presented as embodied in a person or persons", i.e. the restraining principle and the person in whom it is expressed. Most accept that the Holy Spirit is the Restrainer referred to in this verse. The Holy Spirit, in His omnipotence, holds back the full development of lawlessness and the manifestation of the man of sin. God is still on the throne and His purposes will be brought to fruition in His time. The idea in the expression is of a continual restraining - "only the Restrainer who now restrains, will continue to restrain". He was restraining the development of lawlessness when Paul wrote this epistle and has continued to restrain and will continue to restrain until God's appointed time.

"until he be taken out of the way." This expression has been considered the most difficult in the epistle. The word translated 'taken' (*ginomai*) means 'cause to be' or 'to become' and is translated a number of ways in the New Testament. It is translated 'came' and 'shewed' in the first letter (1.5). It is also translated 'ariseth' (Matt 13.21; Mark 4.17). However a strong case has been made for it to indicate the removal of the Restrainer out of the way. The word translated 'way' (*mesos*) is an adjective denoting middle or midst (*cf.* Luke 22.55; John 1.26). Many Commentators believe this expression refers to the Holy Spirit being removed out of the midst of the Church at the event of the rapture. T. Smith states, "The revealing of the man of lawlessness is hindered by the continued presence on earth of believers of the Church period, and the secret working of lawlessness is held back by the presence on earth, and in the believer, of the Holy Spirit, both must be taken out of the way before the man of lawlessness is revealed. The event which will effect this is the Rapture," However, the same difficulty occurs here as in the previous verse in relation to the time note in v.8 which indicates that the Restrainer of this verse and the restraint of v.6 continues up until the man of sin is revealed which is at least 3 1/2 years after the rapture has taken place. An alternative rendering of the expression is "until he ariseth out of the midst" referring back to the last clause of v.6 instead of to the Restrainer. This would indicate that the Holy Spirit would continue to hinder until the appointed time for the antichrist to arise out of the midst of the nations. This would avoid the problem of the Holy Spirit's removal at the rapture and would link with the opening expression of v.8. There are difficulties in both views and one refrains from being dogmatic.

Verse 8. "And then shall that wicked be revealed," The word 'then' refers to a definite point in time indicating that immediately the restraint and the restrainer are withdrawn that wicked will be revealed. Since there is a definite article before the word translated 'wicked' and it means 'lawless' it refers to a person - the lawless one. This is the third title for the antichrist in these verses - As to his character he is the man of sin, as to his destiny he is the man of perdition and as to his activity he is the lawless one. Lawlessness, in all its fullness, will be manifest in a man. It is suggested that the repetition of the word revealed (*apokalupto*) seeks to emphasise the supernatural activity involved in this event. The world will see in this man the sum of all they desire and will think that he will provide all for which they long. Thus they will worship him.

"whom the Lord will consume" The immediate change from the manifestation to the destruction of the antichrist emphasises that Paul's letter was not intended to deal with his reign of lawlessness, but simply to encourage the saints by showing that no power could prevail against the purpose of God. It also indicates that this event was different in time and character to the rapture. The purpose of the rapture was to remove the saints away from the coming wrath (1 Thess 1.10) whereas this event was part of the wrath of God poured out upon the earth. The word translated 'consume' (*analisko*) means 'to use up' or 'to destroy'. The same thought is used in relation to his dominion - "they shall take away his dominion, to consume and destroy it" (Dan 7.26). Here the manifestation of Christ would remove the man of sin and lawlessness from the world.

"with the spirit of his mouth." Here the word 'spirit' can be translated 'mouth'. The same idea is found in Rev 19.15, "out of his mouth goeth a sharp sword, that with it he shall smite the nations." The expression is a quotation from Isaiah 11.4 "with the breath of his lips shall he slay the wicked (or wicked one)." Here, as in Isaiah, it indicates the authoritative utterance of the Judge who comes to take dealings with the earth. It has been pointed out that the thought here is different to Rev 19.15 where the Lord is characterised as the Mighty Warrior. Here the idea is of His power to discharge rapid judgment, although judgment is included in the passage in Rev 19. The expression here manifests the ease with which the Lord Jesus Christ will deal with the one who exalted himself above all and opposed all that is of God. This will be the fulfilment of Num 24.24 "he shall perish for ever", Dan 8.25 "he shall be broken without hand", Dan 9.27 "that determined shall be poured upon the desolate (desolator)" and Dan 11.45 "he shall come to his end, and none shall help him". We know that many believe that these references do not refer to the same person but we do. This man is going to have supremacy over the world. There cannot be another power that is equal to him for he is Satan's supreme man. Our blessed Lord is God's supreme man, the Supreme Man, the true King Priest. The Lord has many titles and fills perfectly many offices. Satan's counterfeit has many descriptions and titles, and will have many offices.

"and shall destroy" The word translated 'destroy' (*katargeo*) means 'to be rendered entirely idle' or 'to reduce to inactivity'. The man of sin, the blasphemer of God, will be struck dumb and powerless. The One he denied and cursed will come and he will be rendered helpless. The indignation of the God he provoked will be upon him and the plan and purpose of Satan will be crushed.

"with the brightness of his coming:" The word translated 'brightness' (*epiphaneia*) means 'shining forth' and the word translated 'coming' means 'presence'- thus the outshining of His presence. Here we have the appearance of the Lord in all His majesty, power and glory. The glorious revelation of the Lord Jesus Christ will immediately destroy and bring to naught the man of sin and all that is associated with him. The antichrist has a revelation (vv.3, 6, 8) and a presence (v.9), but never an *epiphaneia* - an outshining of majesty and glory.

Verse 9. "Even him," These words are not in the Greek text, but they are inserted for connection, meaning the lawless one. Although the apostle has already described the ease with which he will be destroyed, in this verse Paul goes back to the coming of the man of sin in order to give further details concerning him. He goes on to show the hidden power behind his coming and the means used to attract men to him.

"whose coming" Again the word translated 'coming' is *parousia* meaning 'presence' which indicates the period between his revelation and the moment he is brought to naught and removed from the scene.

"is after the working of Satan" The preposition translated 'after' (*kata*) meaning 'according to' refers not only to the moral principle but also to the source. It indicates that Satan will bring in 'his man', the man of lawlessness, and that his presence will be characterised by unrighteousness and rebellion against God. Today many deny the existence of the devil which only demonstrates the ignorance and unbelief of people generally. The Scriptures not only affirm his existence, but also his power. They are both seen in the opening chapters of Job and in the temptation of the Lord Jesus Christ. His power is also revealed in the miracles of the Egyptian magicians. The devil has always been working to discredit the Word of God. The word translated 'working' (*energeia*) means 'energy' and indicates power in action. Here it refers to the ability of Satan. The expression 'according to the working' is found also in Eph 1.19 where it refers to the might of the power of God in raising the Lord Jesus from among the dead. Here we have Satan's counterfeit of that. Instead of the working of divine power we have the operation of satanic power. However we must remember that Satan can do nothing except that which God allows. The emphasis here is upon the power behind the reign of the antichrist. "The dragon gave him his power, and his seat, and great authority" (Rev 13.2). His power - might to accomplish his plan; his seat (throne) - royal dignity and outward splendour; and his authority - legal power. "His power shall be mighty, but not by his own power" (Dan 8.24) - empowered by Satan. All will be in harmony with the devil's plan.

"with all power and signs and lying wonders," The force of the opening words 'with all' is expressed in the words 'in every kind of' indicating the diversity of the working of Satan. It has been stated that there is no grammatical reason why the word 'lying' (*pseudos* - falsehood) should not be linked with the three words 'power, signs and wonders'. W.E.Vine states, "The words may be paraphrased: 'with a display of every kind of power, that is to say, with signs and wonders calculated to deceive,". They refer to the same events but from different standpoints. 'Power' is strength in operation, the supernatural source and means; 'signs' is what is signified, the purpose or indication of the supernatural power; and 'wonders' the result of the signs, causing the beholders to be amazed and convincing them that something exceptional has taken place. These three words which are used of the miracles of the Lord Jesus (Acts 2.22) would characterise false christs and false prophets, (Matt 24.24). The word 'falsehood' does not indicate that the signs or miracles will not be real, i.e. produced by trickery, but that the purpose of them will be to deceive the people into accepting the false claims of the man of sin. They will be signs and wonders calculated to deceive. Here we have the means whereby men are duped into receiving the antichrist and willingly worshiping him. We know that many take this verse as proof that the second beast of Rev 13 is the subject of this chapter. However the verse does not state that the man of sin performs the signs and wonders, but that his presence will be according to the working of Satan. The agent Satan will use is no doubt the second beast - "And he exerciseth all the power of the first beast before him, and causeth the earth and them which dwell within to worship the first beast, whose deadly wound was healed. And he doeth great wonders, so that he maketh fire come down from heaven on the earth in the sight of men, And deceiveth them that dwell on the earth by the means of those miracles which he had power to do in the sight of the beast; ...." (Rev 13. 12-14). Thus both beasts of Rev 13 are referred to in this passage - the first in vv.3-8 and the second in v.9. The first will be prominent, claiming to be God and the second will deceive men in order to direct worship to the first and his image (Rev 13.15).

Verse 10. "And with all deceivableness of unrighteousness" This verse explains the falsehood of the previous verse as well as continuing its theme of deceit. The word 'all' again has the idea of 'every kind', i.e. "every kind of deceit". The devil will use every means to deceive men. He has been seeking to do this through the ages, blinding men as to the truth, but here there will be no restraint as by word and deed, with craftiness and subtlety, without scruple he will deceive men. The character of such deceit will be unrighteousness which is the active power of wrongdoing. Such deceit is clearly seen in the activities of Satan's agent (Rev 13.11-18), but will also be seen in men generally as the next expression implies.

"in them that perish;" The tense of the verb translated 'perish' (*apollumi*), present continuous, is the same as in 1 Cor 1.18 and thus it is literally "in the perishing ones". Falsehood and unrighteousness will be operative in and for those who are perishing. The corresponding noun '*apoleia*' translated 'perdition' (v.3) describes the destiny of the man of sin, thus the tense of the verb here implies that they are already on the road to perdition. They will share a common character with the antichrist and a common doom.

"because they received not the love of the truth," The word 'because' introduces the reason they are perishing and why they are willingly deceived. "Received not" indicates a deliberate and definite rejection of the truth. It corresponds with the expression " obey not the gospel of our Lord Jesus Christ." in chapter 1.8 and is in contrast to the statement in the first epistle, "ye received the word of God" (1 Thess 2.13). There is a principle here - where truth is loved it can be learned, but where there is no love for the truth there will be love for the false. Love for the truth will deliver one from the delusion of the devil. Here the truth will not suit their unrighteous delights and so they will reject it. Today the truth of the gospel is not palatable to most people for they love their own way of life and the pleasures of sin, so they refuse or reject it. Their refusal of Christ opens the door to the deceit of Satan. The attitude of people to the truth of God manifests what they are and determines their eternal destiny. We can make an application of this to the Christian and state that the believer's attitude to the Word of God determines his/her spiritual condition.

"that they might be saved." The rejection of the truth leaves them ignorant of their danger and of the only way of deliverance from coming judgment. They will not endure sound teaching so will turn to falsehood (*cf*, 2 Tim 4.3). Being deluded they will say "peace and safety" only to be overtaken by judgment (1 Thess 5.3) and cry "The harvest is past, the summer is ended, and we are not saved." (Jer 8.20). The door was open for them to receive the truth, the way of God's salvation, but they closed it and thus will become the objects of the vengeance of God. They will make their choice and miss God's salvation. How solemn to neglect God's way of salvation (Heb 2.3) and to reject the message of the gospel.

Verse 11. "And for this cause" The reason given for what follows was their refusal of the truth, their love of darkness rather than light - "And this is the condemnation, that light is come into the world, and men loved darkness rather than light, because their deeds were evil." (John 3.19). In spite of God's desire that all men be saved and come into the knowledge of truth (1 Tim 2.4) they will reject God's offer of salvation, spurn His love, trample under foot the work of Christ and choose falsehood. They never desired the message of the gospel though it was the truth and the door to salvation, but they received and delighted in error since it suited their wicked and deceitful hearts (Jer 17.9).

"God shall send them strong delusion," The Greek verb is in the present tense. However, it does not refer to a present action, but rather to a moral principle. Although this principle is operative at all times, here it refers to a future, to the day of the Lord, thus the AV translation "shall send". Here it is not the case of God allowing them, the perishing, to be deluded, but the principle of God sending them the desire of their hearts. God gives them what they have chosen. This principle is seen throughout the Scriptures:- Pharaoh hardened his heart (Exod 7.22; 8.32) and then the Lord hardened his heart (Exod 9.12); God gave the Israelites their request in the wilderness for flesh and sent leanness into their souls (Ps 106.15; *cf.* Ps 78.29-31); because men not glorify God and changed the truth of God into a lie God gave them up to vile affections, and because they did not like to retain God in their knowledge He gave them over to a reprobate mind (Rom 1.21-32). "God is not mocked: for whatsoever a man soweth, that shall he also reap." (Gal 6.7). Their rejection of the truth will leave God free to act in righteous judicial government. This will not be the final judicial act of God which is judgment, but leads to it as the following verse indicates.

The word translated 'strong' is the same word translated 'working' in v.9 and indicates activity. It is used of the working of the power of God in raising Christ from among the dead (Eph 1.19) and of the working of the power of the Lord Jesus Christ in changing the believer's body at the rapture (Phil 3.21). The word translated 'delusion' (*plane*) is mainly translated 'error' (Rom 1.27; 2 Pet 2.18; 3.17; 1 John 4.6) although it is translated 'deceit' in the first epistle (2.3). Thus the expression 'strong delusion' means 'a working of error' or 'an energy of deceit' indicating that those perishing will receive every form of error.

"that they should believe a lie:" Literally "for to believe the lie". So the intended result in sending them a working of error is the believing of the lie. They, as it were, pull the blind partially down and God pulls it the rest of the way. The lie refers back to v.4 which describes the man of sin, in his impious self-exaltation, claiming to be God. This is the ultimate aim of humanism. The lie is the plan of Satan in setting up the false Christ as God, against

the true Christ, the Son of God, God manifest in the flesh. We can also consider that the antichrist himself is the lie, willingly received by the perishing ones, in contrast to the Lord Jesus Christ, the truth (John 14.6).

Verse 12. "That they might be damned" Here we have the result of their unbelief and the outcome of the working of error in their lives. The ultimate end of believing the lie is damnation. The word translated 'damned' (*krino*) primarily means to distinguish and judicially to judge or pass sentence. It is generally translated 'judge', but here the end result is in view as in v.8. Their acceptance of what is false results in eternal damnation. Man fixed in hatred of God and His word are righteously punished.

"who believed not the truth," It has been stated that this expression is stronger than just 'not believing', but rather indicates a positive rejection of the truth of God. God, in His wondrous grace, sends His truth, through the gospel, that all men might believe and be saved (1 Tim 2.4), for He is not desirous that any should perish (2 Pet 3.9). Through the work of the Lord Jesus Christ on the cross there is provision for all to be saved (1 Tim 2.6), but all will not accept God's salvation despite His longsuffering. Here there is a deliberate rejection of the truth, a blasphemous refusal of God and His Christ and acceptance of the antichrist.

"but had pleasure in unrighteousness." The wickedness of the perishing ones is not just unbelief but moral in their love of evil. They gladly and fully accept the man of sin, the Pretender, because of his impious pretensions in seating himself in the temple as God. The word translated 'pleasure' (*eudokeo*) means 'to think well of', 'approve of' or 'delight in' and is generally used in a good sense. This is the only occasion in which it is used in a bad sense. Their hatred of the truth leads to their delight in unrighteousness. The deceit of unrighteousness in v.10 now becomes delight in unrighteousness. They are delighted that God, the Lord Jesus Christ and the Word of God have all been set aside or replaced, as they imagine, by the antichrist who claims to be God. Instead of rejecting the false and blasphemous claims of the man of sin they rejoice at this diabolical usurpation. They readily accept his laws thinking they were set free from the righteous law of God and are therefore no longer responsible to Him. Having turned their backs on the light they turn to the sphere of darkness yielding themselves to the working of error. This becomes their permanent state and, delighting in unrighteousness, they willingly co-operate with it until at last they are overcome by the righteous judgment of God. In this verse the heart of man, far apart from the truth of God, fully revealed. Christians should appreciate that the flesh in them is always opposed to God and His word. Christians must allow the truth of God to mold their lives, "yielding their members to righteousness unto holiness." (Rom 6.17-19).

Verses 13-17 Concerning the Thessalonians.
These verses are a complete change to what has gone before. Instead of continuing with God's dealings with the world and 'the man of sin' in the day of the Lord, the apostle now turns to God's dealings with His own people in this present day of grace. In vv.13-15 we have Paul's thanksgiving for the saints in Thessalonica and in vv.16-17 we have Paul's prayer for them.

Verses 13-15 Paul gives Thanks for the Saints.
This is a lovely passage that takes in God's programme for His own in contrast with Satan's program in the previous passage. That programme is short and ends in destruction whereas God's program for the saints of this dispensation of grace is over a long period and ends in glory. The saints of today are in God's purposes and counsels of grace and everything is in perfect order in relation to them.

Verse 13. "But we are bound to give thanks alway to God for you," 'But' indicates and introduces a contrast to the judgment of the 'man of sin' and the damnation of his followers. Here Paul feels a deep gratitude as he sees the Thessalonian saints in the great program of God's salvation. He acknowledges that he owed a dept of thanksgiving to God. As in 1.3 the word translated 'bound' (*opheilo*) means to owe a dept to be paid or to have an obligation to be carried out. It indicates a responsibility and is translated 'duty' in Luke 17.10, "we have done that which was our duty to

do."(*cf*. Rom 15.27) and 'due' in 1 Corinthians 7.3, "Let the husband render unto the wife due benevolence:" (*cf*. Matt 18.34). The word translated 'alway' (*pantote*) is generally translated 'always' as in 1.3, 11 and means 'at all times'. It is translated in the first epistle 4.17 'ever, "so shall we ever be with the Lord" (*cf*.5.15) and in 5.16 'evermore, "Rejoice evermore". It indicates that which is continual. The word translated 'thanks' (*eucharisto*) has the idea of willing and joyful thanksgiving to God. As the people of God we ought to constantly and joyfully render thanksgiving to God, not only because of His wondrous grace and great plan of salvation, but primarily for what He is in Himself as well as for all that He has bountifully bestowed upon us.

"brethren beloved of the Lord," The title 'Lord' refers to the Lord Jesus Christ as it does in the whole of the epistle. The relationship of the saints was that of brethren in the same family of God and possessing the same eternal life. The term indicates the same origin as being born of God (1 John 5.1). The were the object of the love of the Lord who had purchased them with His own precious blood (1 Cor6.20). That love is eternal and nothing can separate the believers from it (Rom 8.35-39). In that passage we note that the Love of Christ is also the love of God. We should be constantly in the enjoyment of that love which never fails and can never fade.

> No love can compare,
> With the love of Christ our Saviour,
> Always and ever the same faithful Friend;
> Has He not promised He never will leave thee,
> Lo, I am with you, e'en unto the end.

"Because God hath from the beginning chosen you" The word translated 'because' (*hoti*) is translated 'for that' in v.3 and here introduces the reason for the thanksgiving of Paul and his fellow servants who laboured with him in Thessolanica. The word translated 'chosen'(*haireomai*) has the thought of choosing for one's self. It is only found elsewhere in Philippians 1.22 and Hebrews 11.25 of human choice, However it is also found in the Septuagint (the Greek Old Testament) in Deuteronomy 7.6-7. The usual Greek words used for election are *eklectos* (1 Pet 1.2) and *eclegomia* (Eph 1.4) and the Greek word for predestination is *prooridzo* (Eph 1.5). There are three different views in regard to the expression "from the beginning":-

(1) It refers to the timeless past before creation came into being. Thus God's eternal counsels are in view. T.W. Smith states it "takes us back into the era "from everlasting"; and "It is obviously wrong to limit God's sovereign choice to any point in time,". It is true that one cannot limit God in His sovereign choice whether before or after creation.

(2) The 'beginning' refers to the time when Paul went to Thessalonica with the gospel. To the beginning of his preaching when the Thessalonians believed. The expression 'from the beginning' is also found in 1 John 1.1 which, in the context, seems to refer to the beginning of the public ministry of the Lord Jesus Christ. It was from that time that the disciples heard and saw etc.

(3) Instead of "from the beginning" the expression should be "as firstfruits". W.E.Vine states, "There is, however, an alternative reading, which is well supported and gives a good sense. This is *aparchen (aparche)* = 'first fruits.'......... The term is applied ...... to the earliest believers in a country in relation to those of their countrymen who believe later, Rom 16.5, 1 Cor 16.15."

None of these views set aside the sovereignty of God which is clearly taught in the Word of God. We do not intend to enter into the subject of election which seems to have divided Christians for centuries and seems to have become contentious these days. The Scriptures clearly teaches the sovereignty of God and human responsibility. The puny mind of men cannot fully grasp such a subject - "O the depth of the riches both of the wisdom and knowledge of God! How unsearchable are his judgments, and his ways past finding out!" (Rom 11.33).

"To salvation" What salvation is in view here? Some view it as salvation in its fullness, i.e. past, present and future. Others take it as salvation from wrath in the day of the Lord as in the first epistle (1.10; 5.9). The context would indicate that there is a contrast between the previous verse where we have the damnation of those who believed not the truth and this verse where we have the salvation of those who believe the truth. The future and final salvation seems to be in view which includes deliverance from coming wrath at the rapture. No genuine believer in this day of grace will pass through the great tribulation.

"Through sanctification of the Spirit and belief of the truth." In the sanctification of the Spirit we have the divine side and in the belief of the truth we have the human side. The Spirit is the agent in setting apart to God and from the world. We notice in this verse the mention of each Person in the Trinity - God, the Lord and the Spirit. There is no definite article before the word 'truth' thus the expression is really 'belief of truth. The absence of the article indicates that the moral character and quality of truth is in view. The Holy Spirit enlightens the darkened mind to truth.

Verse 14 "Whereunto he called you" The thought here is 'into which salvation He called you'. The word translated 'called' (*kaleo*) means to call with an object in view. It is, like the word choose in v.13, in the point tense (aorist tense) which indicates a single or once for all act. Here it refers to a point in time when the Thessalonians responded positively to the message of the gospel. This is a contrast to the same word in the first epistle which is in the present continuous tense indicating that God had called and continued to call them unto His kingdom and glory (1 Thess 2.12).

"by our gospel" This expression does not indicate that there were other genuine gospels, but that it was the message which Paul and his fellow servants brought and proclaimed to them. There is but one genuine gospel, i.e. good news from God to men. It is called the gospel of God (1 Thess 2.2) indicating its origin is in God. Since it comes from God men need to take heed to the message. It is called the gospel of Christ (Rom 1.16) because He is its theme, its subject and substance; the gospel of peace (Rom 10.15) revealing how the sinner can have peace with God; the gospel of the grace of God (Acts 20.24) showing the basis of the message is the unmerited love and mercy of God; and the gospel of your salvation (Eph 1.30) indicating the power and product of the message in the lives of those who believe. It was entrusted to Paul (Gal 2.7; 1 Tim 1.11). The message was his and his fellow workers to proclaim and through this message God called them and still calls men.

"to the obtaining of glory" Here the end is in view. Although the Greek word translated 'obtaining' (*peripoiesis*) contains the idea of 'possessing' here the thought is the act of obtaining. It is looking forward to a future day. The word 'glory' covers a wide range of meaning including 'honour' (Jn 5.41, 44), 'praise' (Jn 9.24) and 'dignity' (2 Pet 2.10). It is described as the outward expression of what is inward and essential, thus it takes various forms. It is used of the display of the differing attributes of God.

"of our Lord Jesus Christ." The glory mentioned here cannot be the glory of His deity. It is rather His glory as the Redeemer who finished the work His Father gave Him to do (Jn 17.4) and the glory God gave Him (Acts 3.13; *cf.* Jn 17.22). The reference here is to the glory of the manifestation of Christ in which the believers will share (Col 3.4; *cf.* Phil 3.21). It is the glory mentioned in Romans 8.18 and 2 Corinthians 4.17. This glory we have been called to is eternal (1 Pet 5.10).

Verse 15 "Therefore, brethren, stand fast," The apostle now states the practical conclusion of vv.13-14. In view of the facts stated in regard to their salvation and the certainty of future glory Paul calls upon them to stand fast. He again uses the term 'brethren' reminding them of his care for them and their close relationship to him. There was no need to fear men for their future was secure and they should live in the light of divine purpose. Instead of being soon shaken (v.2), they were to stand firm, having been assured of God's programme. One cannot be distressed or disturbed in mind without it affecting the life. There was no need to fear 'the day of the Lord' since they were in God's plan and their portion was future glory. They were to stand firm continually in their faith and in the assurance of their salvation.

"and hold the traditions which ye have been taught," The word translated 'hold' (*krateo*) is also translated 'take' (Mt 22.6) and 'keep' (Jn 20.23). It means to be strong, keeping a firm grip upon something whether physically (Mt 26.48, Mk 5.41) or mentally (Mk 7.3-4, 8). It is used of keeping the sayings of the Lord (Mk 9.10), of holding fast one's profession (Heb 4.14) & the Lord's name (Rev 2.13). The word for 'traditions' (*paradosis*) means 'what is transmitted or handed down'. It is used in a bad sense of the Jewish Rabbis' teaching (Mk 7.5; elders) which transgressed the commandment of God (Mt 15.3-6) and is referred to by the Lord as the doctrines and commandments of men (Mk 7.7-8). It is also used by Paul to refer to the traditions of my fathers (Gal 1.14). It is used here of the faith once delivered unto the saints (Jude 3). In this sense it refers to the divinely inspired Word of God and indicates that what was being conveyed was from God Himself. The same idea is seen in 1 Thessalonians 2.13 when the Thessalonians accepted the message of the gospel, not as coming from men, although preached by them, but as having it source in God. It could be that the whole Apostolic teaching is in view. Whereas the Apostolic doctrine (teaching) in Acts 2.42 was verbal and partial, in the New Testament it is complete and permanent. It is the important inspired instruction that builds and beautifies Christian character. Believers today should hold fast the divine truth and principles.

"whether by word, or our epistle." oral or written instruction. The oral teaching would refer to that given by the apostle when with them (*cf.* V.5). "Our epistle" refers to Paul's first epistle to them. His written teaching was not distinct or opposite to his oral ministry, but rather substantiated and in one sense replaced it. All of the oral teaching in enshrined in the written Word of God. There is no inspired oral teaching today. The only authority for the Christian today is the Holy Scriptures, the Bible. In the Word of God we have the vital and valuable teaching that guides and guards the child of God. Its teaching is permanent and circumstances or conditions cannot change it.

Vv.16-17 Paul Commends the Saints to God.
Here we have the longing of the apostle that the Thessalonian saints be comforted and established by both the Lord Jesus Christ and the Father in contrast to being shaken by false teaching and thus being trouble at the commencement of the chapter.

Verse 16 "Now" This word gives stress to what follows. As in the first epistle (3.11) the apostle gives expression to his desire and prayer for the saints in Thessalonica. He is here adding prayer to his exhortation in v.15. The word and prayer are linked together (*cf.* Acts 6.4).

"our Lord Jesus Christ himself," The order here is opposite to 1 Thessalonians 3.11 where God is placed first. The reason seems to be that there God is the subject in the preceding verses whereas here the Lord Jesus Christ is the subject in the previous verse. The word 'himself,' is added to either emphasise His present ministry as comforter or to emphasise the contrast between Him and the man of sin, the antichrist in the previous section of the chapter. The Lord Jesus Christ is the One to whom all the saints belong and He cares for each one.

"and God, even our Father," The mention of the Son and the Father together indicates their equality and also their unity and harmony. Thus the deity of the Lord Jesus Christ is implied. The Father and the Son are co-equal and co-eternal each one possessing all the attributes of deity. Here Paul is reminding the saints of their relationship with God into which the grace of God had brought them. The almighty and eternal God was their Father as well as his and the Father of all believers.

"which hath loved us," The verb 'loved' (*agapao*) is in the aorist or point tense, i.e. 'Having loved us', and refers to that love which is eternal, unchanging and unmeasurable. The verb is in the singular and thus some have taken it to refer only to God, even our Father. However, it could be viewed in relation to the oneness of the Father and the Son. W.E.Vine states, "it is perhaps better to take it as referring to both,". It takes us back to the greatest display of that love at Calvary where God gave His Son and the Son willingly laid down His life (Jn 3.16; 13.1). This reference to the love of God (Father and Son) gives them another assurance of their salvation and is an incentive to stand fast.

"and hath given us everlasting consolation," The word 'given' is also in the aorist tense, i.e. 'Having given us'. It seems to point back to when one received the message of the gospel. The word translated 'consolation' (*paraklesis*) is translated 'exhortation' in the first epistle (2.3). Both ideas are embraced in the word. It has the thought of a calling to one's side for comfort and encouragement. It has the idea of calming the mind in times of trouble and anxiety, and of exhorting one to continue in the truth of God. The word 'everlasting' or 'eternal' in this context gives quality to the consolation. It indicates that it is unchanging and unshakeable since it comes from the God of all comfort (2 Cor 1.3).

"and good hope through grace." It has been said that 'consolation' is for our present condition, good hope is the certainty we have of future blessing and glory (*cf.* 1 Thess 1.10; Tit 2.13). The hope is good, not only because of what the future holds for the believer, but also because it sustains, encourages and cheers the saint in the pilgrim pathway now. That hope is called a 'living hope' in 1 Peter 1.3. The basis of that hope is the new life received at new birth. That life characterises the hope which cannot be extinguished by circumstances. It has its origin in God and its certainty in the resurrection of Christ.

Verse 17 "Comfort your hearts," This is in contrast to troubled and shaken minds earlier in the chapter. If the heart is right all else will fall into place - ""Keep thy heart with all diligence; for out of it are the issues of life." (Prov 4.23). The word for comfort is the verbal form of the word translated 'consolation' in v.16. It contains the ideas of consolation, exhortation, encouragement and strengthen. Christians need to be consoled in times of distress, exhorted and encouraged in times of apathy and departure and strengthened in times of difficulty.

"and stablish you in every good word and work." The word translated 'stablish' (*sterizo*) means 'to support, strengthen or confirm'. The thought here seems to be that of strengthening them in what they had been taught by Paul and its application to their lives. It includes their speech and how they lived. It embraces the whole Christian behaviour. It is important to have a knowledge of the Word of God, but knowledge in itself is not enough. Knowledge of the Scriptures should develop Christlikeness in our lives. Spiritual intelligence is intended to produce a manner of life that is worthy of, and pleasurable to, God. Our walk (manner of life) should be worthy of the Lord (Col 1.10), of God (1 Thess 2.12) and of our calling (Eph 4.1). God is able to steady the minds and hearts of His people and leave them steadfast in the midst of the storms of life.

The Day of the Lord and its Application - Practical

If in chapter 1 we have the revelation of Christ and in chapter 2 we have the rebellion of the man of sin, in this chapter we have the responsibility of the saints. In chapter 1 the apostle is confronting the persecutors of the saints, in chapter 2 he is contradicting the false teachers and in this chapter he is challenging the disorderly element in the assembly at Thessalonica. Chapter 3 is the practical part of the epistle which unfolds the responsibility of Christians. It deals with basic Christian living, Christian behaviour and practice, and calls for obedience to the word and will of God. The future events unfolded in the previous chapters are intended to have a practical effect on the saints. The knowledge of future events should have an effect upon our present lives -

"Seeing then that all these things shall be dissolved, what manner of persons ought ye to be in all holy conversation and godliness," (1 Pet 3.11). In the opening verses of the chapter Paul requests the prayer of the Thessalonian believers (vv.1-2). He then states his confidence in them (vv.3-5), yet manifests his concern about the disorderly (vv.6-15). There was evidence of extraordinary conduct in a minority of the saints in the assembly. The apostle closes the epistle with his benediction.

Verses 1-2 Paul's Call or Request to the Saints.
Verse 1. "Finally, brethren," The Greek word translated 'finally' (*loipon*) indicates that there is something remaining and is translated 'remaineth' in 1 Cor 7.29. It does not always indicate the concluding remarks (*cf.* 1 Cor 1.16 translated 'besides', 1 Cor 4.2 translated 'moreover', and Eph 4.14 translated

'henceforth'). It is used here to emphasise and strengthen the practical teaching which remains to be given (*cf.* I Thess 4.1 translated 'further more'). For the fifth time, in this epistle, the apostle uses the term 'brethren' indicating that he was addressing them as brethren in the Lord. Any appeal and admonition that follows is given out of brotherly love and for their spiritual welfare. His affection for the Thessalonian saints is demonstrated by his care and concern for them - "Faithful are the wounds of a friend; but the kisses of an enemy are deceitful." (Prov 27.6).

"pray for us," A key note of most of Paul's epistles was to remind the saints of his constant prayer for them, "Always in every prayer of mine for you all making request with joy," (Phil 1.4; *cf.* Col 1.3; 1 Thess 1.2; 2 Thess 1.11); to request their prayers, "Brethren, pray for us." (1 Thess 5.25; *cf.* Rom 15.30; 2 Cor 1.11; Eph 6.19; Col 4.3) and to encourage them to pray, "Pray without ceasing." (1 Thess 5.17; *cf.* Rom 12.12; Eph 6.15; Phil 4.6; Col 4.2). Prayer is essential to the Christian life, "Men ought always to pray, and not to faint;" (Luke 18.1). The apostle appreciated the prayers of the saints and his request was an indication that he was completely dependant on God. Believers should pray for each other and particularly for those engaged in the Lord's work or those in adverse circumstances. This activity strengthens one's spirituality and, through occupation with the needs of others, self is put aside. Of course one needs to pray for one's self as well as other believers and the Christian's prayer life must also embrace unbelievers, "I exhort therefore, that, first of all, supplications, prayers, intercessions, and giving of thanks, be made for all men;" (1 Tim 2.1). Paul's request is twofold, firstly for the messengers and secondly for the message, i.e. what was committed to them. The servants needed to be in the right condition. Without the divine presence and power their labours would be fruitless. This is true today. We must be in touch with God and completely dependant on Him in our Christian life and our labours for Him.

"that the word of the Lord might have free course," The apostle places the word of the Lord before the workers. The particular reason for requesting their prayers was that the word of the Lord, the gospel, might prosper. He was only concerned with the propagation of the gospel, that it might speed on in triumph to the glory of God. It is the Lord's word which is to be proclaimed in His power. The phrase "free course" is translated from the Greek word *trecho* which means 'to run or walk hastily'(*cf*. Matt 28.81 Cor 9.24; Heb 12.1). The present tense of the verb 'run' gives the sense of continually running. This metaphor implies the unhindered and rapid progress of the gospel. Paul was conscious of the urgent need to preach the gospel and he desired that it be unhindered. It seems that he had in mind Corinth, from where he wrote this epistle, and the difficulties he was facing in preaching the gospel. Thus he solicited the prayers of the saints.

"and be glorified," The present tense is also used here indicating a continuous action, i.e.go on being glorified. The idea is of the gospel being glorified as it is received in faith, resulting in the salvation of sinners - "And when the Gentiles heard this, they were glad, and glorified the word of the Lord; and as many as were ordained to eternal life believed." Paul had seen the word of the Lord glorified in Thessalonica (1 Thess 1.5-6) and desired the same result in Corinth.

"even as it is with you: Literally "even as with you". This refers back to 1 Thess 1 showing that the apostle longed for the same freedom and results in the preaching of the gospel in Corinth as there had been in Thessalonica. The gospel, as it were, came running into Thessalonica and had been honoured in its reception there and Paul yearned for the same at Corinth. The Thessalonian believers had received the word in much affliction and with the joy of the Holy Spirit. He was now requesting them to pray that the same would take place in Corinth. The prayers of the Thessalonian saints, no doubt, helped in the development of the work in Corinth and had a part in the resulting blessing there. We see here Paul's confidence in the word and in prayer.

Verse.2 "And that we may be delivered" The conjunction 'and' continues the subject of prayer thus furthering the request of Paul. As mentioned the apostle puts the message first. However the instinct of self-preservation is evident as in Rom 15.30-31, "Now I beseech you, brethren, for the Lord Jesus Christ's sake, and for the love of the Spirit, that ye strive together with me in your prayers to God for me; That I may be delivered from them that do not believe in Judea;". It does not mean that the servants be rescued for their own sakes, but in order that the going forth of the gospel be not hindered. Paul had already received divine assurance of his preservation in Corinth, "Then spoke the Lord to Paul in the night by a vision, Be not afraid, but speak, and hold not thy peace: For I am with thee, and no man shall set on thee to hurt thee:" (Acts 18.9-10). However, this assurance did not prevent him requesting the saints' prayers. W.E.Vine states, "The knowledge of God's will and purpose does not render prayer superfluous, rather it encourages thereto cp. Ezek 36.37."

"from unreasonable and wicked men:" This expression shows the character and conduct of these men. Their features were like those of the man of sin mentioned in chapter 2. They were hostile to the apostle and opposed to the gospel. This hostility to the gospel is with us today and is on the increase in this land, although not to the same degree or extent as in some other countries. The word translated 'unreasonable' (*atopos*) 'out of place' has the idea of improper and perverse. The word translated 'wicked' (*aoneros*) has the thought of bad, evil or malignant. These men were outrageous, hostile, fanatical opponents of the gospel. They were rebellious, vile and opposed to the truth of God. In view of the aorist tense used it is evident that Paul had a particular event in his mind which, more than likely, is recorded in Acts 18. The Thessalonian themselves had already encountered such men (Acts 17). In ch.1.4 the apostle sought to encourage the saints in regard to their persecution, but he was also experiencing persecution himself at Corinth. He had experienced it at Thessalonica and in many other places. It seems evident from Acts 16-19 and 1 Thess 2.14-16 that this opposition and persecution came from the Jews.

"for all men have not faith." Here the reference is to exercised faith and not to 'the faith', the body of truth. This expression gives us the root cause of the character and conduct of these men. If they had believed God and received the message of the gospel they would not have been unreasonable and wicked. It is not the thought that they did not have the capacity to believe and receive the message, but that they would not believe. Not only would they not believe, but they were totally opposed to the gospel and sought to hinder it being proclaimed. There were some Jews who received the message, but in general they were opposed to it (Acts 18.8-8). How few there are today, in this country, who desire to hear the glorious message of the gospel let alone receive it. In these dark and Godless days most people have no thought for eternity and, sad to say, no time for the Saviour our glorious Lord Jesus Christ. The darker the day the more we wonder at the longsuffering of God, not willing that any should perish. However the day of grace will come to and end and the wrath of God will fall upon this world. How good it is to be saved and to know the Saviour.

Verses 3-5 Paul's Confidence in the Saints.
Verse.3 "But the Lord is faithful," This opening expression contrasts the faithfulness of the Lord with the faithlessness of the men in v.2. W.E.Vine states, "in Greek the order is 'not all have faith, faithful, however, is the Lord,'". This emphasises the contrast between the Lord and men. In order to encourage the saints, despite the opposition, the apostle turns to the character of the Lord. He is trustworthy and they could absolutely depend upon Him. There are two reasons why 'the Lord' is mentioned here:- (1) because Paul has been dealing with the day of the Lord and now he has in view the Lord and His people in the day of grace; (2) because this is the practical section and the Lordship of Christ is in view to which the saints ought to bow in obedience to His word.. The apostle had reminded them in his first epistle of divine faithfulness in regard to preservation (5.23-24) and now he reminds them of the Lord's unchanging and unchangeable faithfulness - "He abideth faithful," (2 Tim 2.13). Believers today can rely on His faithfulness for it is the same as when He called us (1 Cor 1.9) and in His faithfulness He will not allow us to be tempted above what we are able to bare (1 Cor 10.13). He is faithful in forgiveness as well as being just (1 John 1.9) and also faithful in His promises (Heb 10.23; 11.11). In these first three verses we see (1) the fellowship of the saints and how precious that is, (2) the hostility of the unregenerate and (3) the faithfulness of the Lord.

"who shall stablish you," The use of the second person 'you' indicates that Paul is turning from his own dangers to the dangers to which the saints were exposed. The word translated 'stablish' (*sterizo*) means to set fast, confirm or strengthen and is used of the Lord when He 'stedfastly set' His face to go to Jerusalem (Luke 9.51). Nothing could divert Him or prevent Him from treading that pathway. The apostle used the word in his first epistle of Timothy's coming to strengthen them (3.2) and of their hearts being stablished (3.13; *cf.* James 5.8). He has already used the word in this epistle stating his desire and prayer for them (2.17). What was a prayer there has become an assurance here showing the confidence of Paul in prayer. He was confident that the Lord would strengthen them and develop in them features like His own in spite of the opposition. The desire of God is that the features seen in the Lord Jesus Christ, in all their perfection, might be increasingly developed in every child of God through the power of the indwelling Holy Spirit. God has the power to establish the saints (Rom 16.25) and He does so in His grace (2 Pet 1.12). It is important for the believer to read and meditate upon the word of God in order to be grounded in the truth so that it might be displayed in one's life.

"and keep you from evil." The apostle now turns to the protection of the saints and the source of the persecution and opposition. The word translated 'keep' (*phulasso*) has the idea of watching or being on guard. Although generally translated 'keep' it is twice translated 'beware', but on both occasions the thought is of guarding, i.e., against covetousness (Luke 12.51) and against being led into error (2 Pet 3.17). This thought is also clearly evident in Acts 12.4. Although the definite article is with the word 'evil' there are different opinions as to its meaning. Some take it as referring to the evil men in v.2, some believe it refers to evil generally and others think Satan is in view. In his first epistle Paul refers to Satan hindering (2.18) and to his fear of the devil tempting them (3.5). In this second epistle he has already mentioned the working of Satan (2.9) and so it is likely that Satan is also referred to here. The apostle is pin pointing the source of the persecution and the pernicious teaching mentioned in the epistle. Paul could see the devil working through the false teachers and in those who were opposed to the gospel, but he could also see the Lord working in the saints. Paul was aware that the Lord alone could guard the saints - ""greater is he that is in you, than he that is in the world." (1 John 4.4).

Verse.4 "And we have confidence in the Lord touching you," The Greek preposition translated 'touching' (*epi*) has the thought of direction, towards, and here implies that the apostle's confidence concerning the Thessalonian saints was in the Lord. What an encouragement this must have been to the saints. His confidence in the saints is the outcome of his confidence in the Lord because He was the source of their strength. The same thought is in Gal 5.10, "I have confidence in you through the Lord,". Paul had confidence in the Lord's people because of their relationship to Him (*cf.* 2 Cor 2.3; 7.16; Philemon 21), but he had no confidence in the flesh (Phil 3.3).

"that ye both do and will do" Although the faithfulness of the Lord is unchanging the Christian is not expected to be passive but characterised by diligence and obedience. The reception of the gospel, trusting the Lord Jesus Christ, is the beginning of a life marked by constant obedience to the Word of God. In Acts 2.41-42 those who received his word continued steadfastly in the apostles' doctrine. We must note the present and future tenses of the verb 'do' indicating that the Thessalonian saints had been doing, and would be doing in the future, what the apostle expected. The faithful conduct of the saints in the past gave Paul assurance that they would continue to be faithful in the future. I wonder if we give this assurance to others by our present behaviour? The apostle is saying "you have done it before and I know you will do it again". It seems as if Paul was referring to the previous chapters and their spiritual growth in spite of the persecution and the false teaching which had shaken them. What was produced in them was produced by the divine power of the Spirit. It is God who plants spiritual desires in us and gives us the power to carry them out - "For it is God which worketh in you both to will and to do of his good pleasure." (Phil 2.13).

"the things which we command you." Having reminded them of the faithfulness of the Lord and mentioned his confidence in their future conduct the apostle tenderly states that it involved obedience to his commandments. These commandments were those given to them when he was with them (1 Thess 4.2), those mentioned in his previous letter and also the instructions given in this epistle. The apostolic authority to command or charge the saints equates with divine revelation, for these apostolic commandments are, in essence, the commandments of the Lord (*cf.* 1 Cor 14.37). The believer, in whole hearted subjection to the Lordship of Christ, should be characterised by full obedience to the Word of God.

Verse 5 "And the Lord direct your hearts" Having mentioned their responsibility, the apostle now desires to direct their hearts elsewhere. He has already pointed out the source of the hostility and opposition, but now he draws their attention to the source of their strength and comfort, God the Father and the Lord Jesus Christ. The word translated 'direct' (*kateuthuno*) which means 'to make straight' or 'to guide'. It is only found elsewhere in the first epistle (3.11) where it refers to the removal of the hindrances preventing Paul from going to Thessalonica, and in Luke 1.79 where it is translated guide. The thought here is of the removal of everything that would rob the saints of being in the good of the love of God and the patience of Christ.

"into the love of God," There is a difference of opinion as to whether this expression refers to God's love for the saints or their love for God. The context favours God's love for them, but probably both are included, i.e. God's love for them would stimulate their love for God. Thus being directed into the atmosphere of God's love would increase their love for Him and this would lead to complete obedience to His word. The more we are in the enjoyment of the love of God the more our love for Him will increase and the more willing we will be to obey the Word of God. "If ye love me, keep my commandments." (John 14.15), "And this is love, that we walk after his commandments." (2 John 6).

"and into the patient waiting for Christ." The word translated 'patient' (*hupomone*) has the thought of constancy, steadfastness or endurance. Some take this expression as referring to the endurance of the Lord Jesus Christ while He was here on earth (Heb 12.2). Thus it would be a pattern for the saints to follow. However, although the word 'waiting' is not in the original Greek text, the idea here is of steadfastly or patiently waiting, referring to the present patience of Christ as He waits, at His Father's right hand. He is waiting for the moment when He will come for His Bride, His purchased possession. The apostle wants the saints to enter into and practice that patience as they wait for the coming of Christ. So believers today should patiently wait for the Lord's imminent coming to take them to be forever with Him. W.E.Vine paraphrases the last two clauses in this way, "the Lord teach and enable you to love as God loves, and to be patient as Christ is patient.".

Verses 6-15 Paul's Concern as to Disorderly Behaviour.
In this section we have the extraordinary behaviour of a minority in the assembly and how to react to it. This minority had not taken heed to the admonition mentioned in the first epistle (5.14) and may have used the truth of the Lord's imminent return as an excuse to continue their laziness. Whereas in the first epistle the apostle admonishes them, here he goes much further and commands them. Thus the background to the epistle is disturbance from without,i.e. persecutors and false teachers, and disturbance from within, i.e. a disloyal minority.

Verse 6 The Apostle's Command.
"Now we command you, brethren," The apostle here turns from the opposition which was coming from without to problems which had arisen from within the assembly. The word for 'command' is the same as in v.4. It is a military term, a charge from a superior officer. The charge is to the assembly regarding how to act towards the unruly minority. However, the firmness of the charge is tempered by Paul's affection for all the saints which is evident in the expression 'brethren' which included the disorderly. He had a deep concern for the spiritual well being of the assembly and its testimony in Thessalonica. The personal conduct of every saint in the assembly is important to the collective testimony in the locality.

What we are positionally, in Christ, should be expressed practically in our lives.

"in the name of our Lord Jesus Christ," The apostle Paul had no inherent authority in himself, his apostolic authority was derived from the Lord. Thus the divine authority of the Lord Jesus Christ was behind his commandment. The Lord's Name stands for all that He is in Himself which includes both His authority and His character. This emphasised the importance of the commandment or charge and showed the gravity of the situation. It was clearly more potent than the exhortation in 1 Thess 5.14 and was intended to have an affect on all the saints in the assembly.

"that ye withdraw yourselves" The word translated 'withdraw' (*stello*) has the thought of 'holding back' or 'holding aloof' from a person. W.E.Vine states it is "a word used of the furling of a sail, and hence, metaphorically, of shrinking from any person or thing:". The word is only found elsewhere in 2 Cor 8.20 where it is translated 'avoid'. There Paul sought to avoid the possibility of suspicion or blame in regard to the collection for the needy saints in Jerusalem. Thus the thought here is not that of excommunication, as is the case of immorality or false teaching, but that of withdrawing from their company and having no part in their behaviour by not supporting them. There was to be a clear disassociation from their behaviour. This is not as strong as Rom 12.17 where the injunction is to turn away from those who caused divisions and acted contrary to doctrine.

"from every brother that walketh disorderly," The adverb translated 'disorderly' (*ataktos*) is only found here and in v.16. It is a military term meaning to be marching out of rank. The verb is only found in v.7 (disorderly) and the adjective is only found in 1 Thess 5.14 (unruly). The context would indicate that there were some who were not marching in line with the teaching of the apostle. This principle can refer to many things. However the following verses indicate that idleness is in view. The disorderly were not conducting themselves in keeping with the Word of God and therefore were out of step with the majority of the assembly.

"and not after the tradition which he (or they) received of us."

As in ch.2.15 the word translated 'tradition' refers to what is transmitted or handed down. It is used in a bad sense of the teaching of the scribes and Pharisees which transgressed the commandment of God (Mt 15.3-6). However it is used in a good sense here of the apostle's teaching which was divinely inspired and are now part of the Holy Scriptures. The Scriptures are the inspired instructions that guide and direct us in the pathway of the will of God.

Verses 7-10 The Example to Follow.

Verse 7. "For yourselves know how ye ought to follow us:" The apostle justified his command by drawing attention to the knowledge which they had obtained by observing the manner of life of Paul and his fellow labourers. They saw the kind of life exemplified that is becoming of a Christian exemplified in the servants. The life of Paul was in keeping with what he taught, he practised what he preached. Believers must practice what they profess to believe as this is vital to their testimony. The verb translated 'ought' (*dei*) means 'it is necessary' or 'one must'. It has the thought of owing a debt and of a duty to be carried out. Paul had commended the Thessalonians in his first epistle for following his example (1.6). Now he desires that they continue to follow him. The word translated 'follow' (*mimeomai*) means to imitate or copy. The apostle had the moral right to call upon the saints to imitate him because he was a devoted imitator of Christ (1 Cor 11.1) and a pattern of selfless and sacrificial service (*cf.* 1 Cor 4.16; Phil 3.17). Believers ought to follow those who are Christ-like in their behaviour.

"for we behaved not ourselves disorderly among you:" Paul is reminding them that they had never seen him or his fellow servants, when they were with them, marching out of step with what they taught. Their behaviour was always in keeping with the tradition they proclaimed. Thus the Christ-like conduct of the apostle was an example they should follow. The initial effect of the preaching of the gospel on these Thessalonian believers was such that they themselves became an example for believers in Macedonia & Achaia to follow (1 Thess1.7). Now they are called upon to imitate the example of the labourers who had brought the gospel to them.

Verse 8. **"Neither did we eat any man's bread for naught;"** The apostle continues the theme of following the example of the servants by reminding the saints that they supported themselves through their own labours. Paul used a Hebraism in the expression "eat bread" which indicates a meal (2 Sam 9.7; *cf*. Ps 41.9; Acts 2.46) and here implies being maintained. The word translated 'naught' (*dorean*) means 'freely', i.e. received as a gift. The Lord used the same word in Matt 10.8, "freely ye have received, freely give." The same sentiment is intended by Paul here as when he used the same word in 2 Cor 11.7.

"but wrought with labour and travail night and day," The labourers supported themselves by constantly toiling physically and mentally. The word for 'labour' (*kopos*) refers to toil that often results in weariness whereas the word for travail (*mochthos*) indicates the pain and stress involved in work. This is emphasised in the expression "night and day" implying steadfastness and consistency. There had been difficulties and opposition for Paul and his fellow servants while at Thessalonica. Three times in Paul's two epistles to the Thessalonians the phrase "night and day" occurs. In 1 Thess 3.9 and also here it is used in relation to the work of the Lord and in 1 Thess 3.10 it is used of wrestling in prayer. Paul also used it regard to his constant warning to the elders of the Ephesian assembly of coming danger (Acts 20.31).

"that we might not be chargeable to any of you:" They deliberately preached the gospel freely by working to support themselves. They would not make a claim upon the Thessalonians to meet their material needs, but laboured to meet the spiritual needs of the saints (1 Thess 2.9). We notice a contrast between this passage and 2 Cor II. Here the apostle had discerned that there were some who were not keen on working. He saw this in their character and thus the servants would not be burdensome to the saints in order to be an example to them as stated in the following verse. In Corinth Paul had detected that there were those who would oppose him and accuse him of being there for material gain, thus Paul would not be burdensome to the Corinthians, in order to prevent such a charge being laid against him. In Thessalonica it was to set an example and in Corinth it was to prevent criticism. The labouring and travailing of the servants was a rebuke to the disorderly and an indication that there was no room for laziness in the Christian life.

Verse 9. "Not because we have not power," This opening expression is intended to verify what has been already stated and to prevent any misconception of the actions taken by the servants. The word translated 'power' (*exousia*) comes from a Greek verb '*exesti*' meaning 'it is lawful'. It is translated 'authority' (Matt 21.23-24; Acts 9.14; 2 Cor 10.8) and 'right' (Heb 13.10; Rev 22.14) and denotes freedom or authority to act in a certain way or take a certain course. Here it could refer to apostolic authority, but it refers primarily to the right of the servants to expect maintenance from the Thessalonian believers. This right to receive maintenance from those among whom they laboured is clearly stated by Paul in 1 Cor 9.1-14 (*cf*. Rom 15.17; 1 Tim 5.18). This principle, which is referred to in the Old Testament is also stated by the Lord Himself (Matt 10.10; Luke 10.7). Having this right the apostle explains the reason why they did not exercise it.

"but to make ourselves an ensample unto you" They willingly set aside their right for the benefit of the assembly. They worked with their own hands (1 Cor 4.12; Eph 4.28), not because they had no other income, for Paul had received two gifts from the assembly in Philippi while he was in Thessalonica (Phil 4.16), but to make themselves an example to the Thessalonian saints. The word translated 'ensample' (*tupos*) carries the idea of a pattern cut out (*cf*. 1 Thess 1.7). They were presenting themselves to the saints as a pattern of the Christian life, serving others. "Look not every man on his own things, but every man also on the things of others. Let this mind be in you ,which was also in Christ Jesus:" (Phil 2.4-5).

"to follow us." The saints were to imitate the labourers, following the pattern cut out for them. The pattern of their manual labours not only proved that they had no material motive in their preaching, but was a condemnation of the slothfulness of some in the assembly. The pattern of their lives was in keeping with their preaching. Both their preaching and their lives were a voice to the saints.

Verse 10. **"For even when we were with you,"** This expression takes us back to the time before Paul wrote his first epistle, to his teaching and his example while he was with them. Thus it embraces the subject of tradition in v.6 and the subject of his example in vv.7-9. It also implies that Paul and his companions took note of the behaviour of those who received the message of the gospel they proclaimed.

"this we commanded you," The Greek participle translated 'even' (*kai*) in the previous expression is generally translated 'also' (2 Thess 2.10). In fact it is translated this way twelve times in the first epistle and twice in this epistle (1.5, 11). Thus here it implies that not only did Paul set them an example, by his conduct among them, and instruct them in the truth of God, but that he also continually commanded them. He had the moral right to do so because he practised what he commanded. It is evident that the apostle had noticed the idle tendency of some of the believers and thus the necessity of the commandment.

"that if any man would not work, neither should he eat." It has been stated that this expression is similar to a saying of the Jewish Rabbis based upon Gen 3.19, "In the sweat of thy face shalt thou eat bread,". The expression "would not work" indicates an attitude or determination of the mind. It refers to those who would not work, not to those who could not work or those who could not get work. Here we have persons who are determined not to work, lazy and indifferent to their moral responsibility. It is normal and natural for men to go out to work. The two negatives in the expression emphasis the moral obligation, no work then no food. Men who can work, but will not work have no consideration or compassion for others. It shows an attitude of selfishness. One is reminded of Paul's words to the Ephesian elders, "I have shown you all things, how that so labouring ye ought to support the weak, and to remember the words of the Lord Jesus, how he said, It is more blessed to give than to receive." (Acts 20.35). Christian workmen ought to be the most willing workmen, putting their all into their work in the light of Col 3.22-23, "Servants, obey in all things your masters according to the flesh, not with eyeservice, as menpleasers, but in singleness of heart, fearing

God: And whatsoever ye do, do it heartedly, as to the Lord, and not unto men;". While the Christian workman ought not to be materialistic, he should be faithful in his work appreciating that in it he is serving the Lord Christ (Col 3.24).

Verses 11-12 The Disorderly Charged and Exhorted.
Verse 11. "For we hear that there are some which walk among you disorderly," Here we have the reason why Paul introduced the subject. The idea is that of the apostle continually hearing of the disorderly minority and thus he does not give the source of his information. It is suggested that the bearer of the tidings which resulted in the writing of this epistle was also the source. The expression 'which walk among you disorderly' may be intended to make those who were idle realise that they were seen as merely being among the saints instead of demonstrating that they were saints. Believers ought to manifest, by their lives, that they are what they claim to be, the children of God.

"Working not at all, but are busybodies." The offenders were idle as to work, yet were active in a wrong way. As a result of their idleness they had developed into busybodies, meddling in the affairs of others. W.E.Vine states that there is a figure of speech here called paronomasia - they were not busy yet were busybodies. There is a danger in idleness as it can develop into less desirable activity, for nature always seeks employment. It is said that from idleness men's disposition passes to curiosity. If there is nothing to occupy the hands there is the danger of seeking something to occupy the tongue. The disorderly were not prepared to be busy in their own business, but were quite prepared to be engaged in the business of others. The Greek participle (*periergazomai*) is only found here in the New Testament and means to work all around, i.e. bustle about or meddle, to be a busybody. A similar adjective (*perierchomai*) is translated 'wandering about' in 1 Tim 3.13, 'wandered about in Heb 11.37 and 'vagabond' (wandering in Newberry Bible margin) in Acts 19.13. T.W.Smith states, "it is of interest, as some commentators point out, that it was "loungers about the market-place" which the Jews used against Paul in Acts 17.5, indicating that a lazy do-nothing type was known in Thessalonica of that day." It seems that the idleness Paul sought

171

to prevent, among the saints in his first epistle (4.11-12; 5.14), was still prevalent. The activity of the disorderly was not conducive to the assembly's well being and testimony. Their initial idleness developed into superfluous chatter, which robbed another's time, and then into mischievously prying into the business of others. Idleness and prying into the business of others is a blight upon one's testimony. It dishonours the Lord and undermines the gospel we proclaim.. It is important that believers in an assembly conduct themselves in a way that will enhance the testimony of God in the locality. The manner of life of the Christian should be "as it becometh the gospel of Christ." (Phil 1.27). "Provide things honest in the sight of all men." (Rom 12.17).

Verse 12. "Now them that are such we command and exhort"
The apostle now addresses the disorderly element in the assembly. He had given a command to the assembly in v.6 to withdraw from those who were walking out of step, now he commands that very company. It is significant that Paul only uses the word translated 'command' (*paranggello*) in this section of the epistle and three times in relation to this subject of idleness (vs.6, 10, 12). He only used it once in his first epistle in regard to the same subject (4.11). This indicates how important the behaviour of the saints is to the well being of the assembly and its collective testimony. The word translated 'exhort' (*parakaleo*) is translated 'comfort' in 2.17 and 'beseech' in 1 Thess 4.10. It contains the thought of drawing alongside to aid and the idea of addressing a person or persons in order to produce a response. Here the apostle encourages them by his exhortation to obey his command and fall into line with the majority of the assembly, by forsaking their idleness and commencing work. The tense suggests urgency in this matter, i.e. he urges them to respond for their own benefit and the benefit of all.

"by our Lord Jesus Christ," Both 'command' and 'exhort' are governed by this expression. Although the command is given with apostolic authority it is modified by this expression which has in view their relationship to the Lord and to Paul as well as to all the saints. Thus the commandment and the exhortation are given in the spirit of love, appealing to the disorderly to respond in the light of that relationship, and because of the honour and Lordship of Christ. The Lordship of Christ demands the obedience of every child of God to the Word of God. That relationship also implies that Christians should consider each other in the bonds of love. We can apply this to the body aspect of the local assembly - "That there should be no schism in the body; but that the members should have the same care one for another. And whether one member suffer, all the members suffer with it; or one member be honoured, all the members rejoice with it." (1 Cor 12.25-26).

"that with quietness they work," The word translated 'quietness' (*hesuchia*) is elsewhere translated 'silence (Acts 22.2; 1 Tim 2.11, 12). It refers to a moral attitude and carries the idea of tranquillity of mind, i.e. laying aside curiosity and living peaceably (*cf.* 1 Thess 5.13). There is a contrast between 'quietness' here and 'busybody' in v.11, that is their busy meddling which might cause strife. There is also a contrast between 'work' here and 'disorderly' in v.11, which refers to their idleness. The exhortation is intended to help them replace a life of meddlesome activity with a quiet consistent life of engagement in one's own business.

"and eat their own bread." They were to provide for themselves and their families. The expression "their own' is emphatic and stresses that they should provide for themselves instead of living off others. The tense indicates that, peacefully working, they will keep on eating their own bread. W.E.Vine states that the rabbinical teaching was not dissimilar to this. "When a man eats his own bread he is of a quiet and orderly turn of mind, whereas if he devours the bread of his parents or children, to say nothing of that of other folks, he is less quietly disposed." The whole verse suggests a manner of life characterized by lawful activity, signifying a calm and contentment which is opposite to the noise of meddling. Believers are to provide for themselves, where possible, and have to give to others thus showing an unselfish attitude. The perfect example of unselfishness is seen in the Lord Himself who came down from the glory on high to meet our need and make us His own. This should be reflected in the lives of all the saints.

Verses 13-15 Concluding Instructions.

Verse 13. **"But ye, brethren,"** The opening word 'but' is in definite contrast to the previous verses. It indicates that the apostle is now turning to address the assembly, with the orderly majority in mind. He affectionately calls upon them to continue on the same course and not be hindered by the behaviour of the disorderly.

"Be not weary in well doing." The verb translated 'weary' (*ekkakeo*) has the thought of being fainthearted, losing heart or lacking courage. It is used by the apostle four other times:- (1) 2 Cor 4.1; Although the apostle experienced trails and persecution he did not faint or become discouraged in carrying out the ministry entrusted to him. Whatever the problems or difficulties in this day of godlessness and departure from the truth of God, Christians should not be discouraged, but seek to live for God and stand for the truth of God outlined in the Word of God; (2) 2 Cor 4.15-16 In spite of burdens, hardship and fatigue, Paul did not become fainthearted because he knew that his preaching increased thanksgiving of many which redounded to the glory of God and because the inward man was renewed daily. Although our bodies are wearing out, we should not be discouraged because of the glory that awaits us. The outward man refers to the physical, but the inward man refers to the spiritual and this is the real person who will experience no decay. The more the outward man wears down, the more the inward man lays hold of that which is eternal; (3) Gal 6.9 The apostle encouraged the Galatian saints not to lose heart in practising what was right in the face of false teachers, for in God's time they would be abundantly recompensed. Believers ought not to be downhearted if there appears to be very little for their labours for the Lord as He alone can righteously assess what has been accomplished. In due time we shall reap, maybe here, but certainly at the Judgement Seat of Christ. We must not be discouraged nor give up but continue in the things of God.; (4) Eph 3.13 Paul expresses his desire that the Ephesian saints be not disheartened because of his sufferings for he was glad to endure tribulation in carrying out his ministry to the Gentiles. Rather they should rejoice in the benefit brought to the Gentiles which was their glory. The only other writer who used the verb in the New Testament was Luke in relation to prayer - "men ought always to pray, and not to faint." (Luke 18.1). Believers should always pray and particularly when there is a tendency to be discouraged or down hearted.

The Greek word translated 'well doing' (*kalopoieo*) only occurs here in the New Testament and means to live virtuously, do what is right, act uprightly. The apostle's appeal was intended to prevent the danger of the orderly reacting to the wrong behaviour of the disorderly. There is a danger of one extreme producing another extreme. If saints see there are lazy folk who are taking advantage of their kindness they could consider cutting off their charity. They should not be discouraged and allow this to happen, but rather do what is right and in keeping with the Word of God instead of being guided by fleshly reactions. Thus Paul is encouraging their charitable works in support of the needy and indicating that they must act in love not in spite or bitterness towards them.

Verse 14. "And if any man obey not our word by this epistle," The apostle turns from the disorderly minority to the individual thus placing responsibility upon each one. The opening statement is the only instance in the New Testament where disobedience of an apostolic command is envisaged. It is evident from Paul's first epistle (4.11) that the apostle had commanded the Thessalonian saints, when he was with them, to engage in their own business and to work with their hands. He had also exhorted them to do so in that epistle. It has been suggested that the disorderly refused to acknowledge the authority of a letter. In using the term "this epistle" Paul is emphasising not only the fact that his epistles carried the same apostolic authority as his spoken word but also that this authority had been disregarded by some. The word translated "obey" (*hupakono*) means to take heed and carry out instructions given. Thus the seriousness of continuing in disobedience is accentuated.

"note that man," The verb translated "note" (*semeioo*) signifies to mark someone or something and being in the continuous tense it means "keep on noting or marking that man". The continuous tense also implies that no hasty conclusion should be made from one action, but that the general conduct should be observed. Since it is also in the middle voice it means to keep on noting that man for yourselves. Some take this personal notation to refer to the Overseers who should be the first to notice a believer walking out of step. However the reference seems to be to the assembly or at least the orderly majority.

"and have no company with him," We note that a different action is called for here to that in v.6. The consequence of continuing disobedience to the apostle's command is greater. First the orderly majority are to withdraw from any disorderly brother (v.6); followed by Paul's example for the saints to imitate (vv.7-10); then the apostle commands and exhorts the disorderly (v.12); now those who disobey the word ought to be isolated. Whereas in v.6 it is withdrawing from, here it is having no company with the disorderly. It is not excommunication as in 1 Cor 5, but social separation from the person. Here it is internal discipline. The compound Greek word translated "have company with" (*sunanamignumi*) is only found again in 1 Cor 5,9, 11 and is translated "company with" (v.9) and "keep company" (v.11). It means 'to mingle' and here indicates having no company or dealings with, no close fellowship in order to have an affect upon the offender.

"that he may be ashamed." Don't behave like him, don't encourage him in his conduct and don't socialise with him. There should be a definite indication of disapproval of his conduct, for his ultimate good, that he might become ashamed. This action may well cause the disorderly brother to ask why one is not so friendly to him. This would give opportunity to tell him that his behaviour has prevented the fellowship which one desired to show and that such behaviour was not in keeping with being a Christian and was harmful to the collective testimony of the assembly. The word translated "ashamed" (*entrepo*) means 'to turn in' and, is translated 'regard' (Luke 18.2, 4) and 'reverence' (Luke 20.13; Heb 12.9). Here, it has the thought of turning on one's self to produce a feeling of shame which results in a change of heart and behaviour.

V.15 "Yet count him not as an enemy," In this verse the apostle is seeking to prevent any harsh feelings towards the disorderly. There is a right manner in which discipline should be carried out. There should be no harshness or legality for that would not accomplish the recovery which is the purpose of the discipline. Discipline should never be carried out in a spirit of bitterness or enmity, but in a spirit of love. The word "enemy" is used in contrast to "brother" in the following statement. A believer may stray, stumble or fall, but having been born of the Spirit he or she is still a child of God and where reproof or discipline is necessary they should still be dealt with as a child of God. The offender here is a believer and thus the discipline has restoration to the mind of God and to the orderly majority in view.

"but admonish him as a brother." The word translated "admonish" (*noutheteo*) means 'to put in mind' and here has the thought of correcting by instruction. W.E.Vine states, "The difference between 'admonish' and 'teach' seems to be that, whereas the former has mainly in view the things that are wrong and call for warning, the latter has to do chiefly with the impartation of positive truth,". The emphasis here is not only on influencing the intellect, but also influencing the will and the disposition. Since the disorderly person is also in the family of God, redeemed with the blood of Christ and precious to Him, he should be treated with brotherly love.

The importance of brotherly love is constantly mentioned in the Scriptures. Brotherly love is the tender affection of family relationship and each one in the family is responsible to manifest it. It is a commandment of the Lord, "This is my commandment, That ye love one another, As I have loved you." (John 15.12; *cf.* John 13.34). We are exhorted to let brotherly love continue (Heb 13.1) and it should be unfeigned, coming out of a pure heart and that fervently (1 Pet 1.22). Brotherly love is an indication of the new life in the believer (1 John 5.1). For his sake and the assembly's benefit treat him tenderly and with feeling for him. Only the assurance of Christian love and care enables the admonition to be received and respected. In all probability, only in this way will the desired end be reached.

Verses 16-18 Paul's Conclusion or Salutation.

Verse 16. "Now" Some question whether this verse has particular reference to the subject the apostle has been dealing with, that is the disorderly element which was disturbing and troubling the assembly; or is he looking back to the persecution and disturbing false teaching which had been mentioned earlier in the epistle. However, the word 'now' seems to indicate that the whole epistle is in view. The word is emphatic and implies a marked contrast to what has gone before. The persecution, false teaching and behaviour of the disorderly element in the assembly would have distressed the saints, but although the circumstances were very disturbing the apostle would have all the believers to enjoy that inward tranquillity which comes from the enjoyment of fellowship with the Lord.

"The Lord of peace himself" The emphasis here is upon the pronoun 'Himself' drawing attention to the One who imparts peace. This title of the Lord is only used here although the title "God of peace" occurs five times in the New Testament (Rom 15.33; 16.20; Phil 4.9; 1 Thess 5.23; Heb 13.20). However, one of the names of the Lord Jesus Christ in Isaiah 9.6 is "The Prince of Peace". He is the embodiment of peace. The One who, because of what He is in Himself, will in a coming day, completely subdue every foe and banish every disturbing element to bring peace to the earth. The true Shiloh (peace maker or pacifier) shall come and unto Him shall the gathering of the people be (Gen 49.10). In that coming day "he shall speak peace unto the heathen: and his dominion shall be from sea even to sea, and from the river even to the ends of the earth." (Zech 9.10).

"give you peace always by all means." The word translated 'peace' (*eirene*) has the thought of spiritual prosperity. It is that tranquillity which comes from living in harmony with God and His word. The idea here seems to be that of harmony and well being. The Lord made peace by the blood of His cross (Col 1.20) and He is our peace (Eph 2.14). When His disciples were troubled He would comfort them saying "My peace "Peace I leave with you, my peace I give unto you: not as the world giveth, give I unto you. Let not your heart be troubles, neither let it be afraid." (John 14.27). The word is used in the opening salutation of all the epistles and the Revelation except 1 John, 3 John and James although it is used in both 2 John and James. Peace is a feature in the character of the Lord and should be displayed in the lives of the saints and particularly in their attitude to each other. We are exhorted "If be possible, as much as lieth in you, live peaceable with all men." (Rom 12.18). We should allow that peace to rule in our lives (Col 3.15) and be peace makers and not trouble makers. If the exhortations of the epistle were heeded and adjustments made so that saints were of the same mind and doing what was right there would be harmony in the assembly. This would be true of assemblies today if the Word of God was heeded and carried out in all our lives. The expression "always by all means" has the thought of continually and in every way.

"The Lord be with you all." The prayer of Paul for the Thessalonian saints was not only that they would enjoy peace but also that they would experience the Lord's presence with them. It is suggested that the apostle's prayer here is based upon the Lord's promise (Mt 18.20) and his own experience - "For I am with thee" (Acts 18.10). To have the assurance of the Lord's presence with them not only brought comfort, but also encouragement and security. We too have the promise of the Lord, "I will never leave thee, nor forsake thee."(Heb 13.5). One notes that the word 'all' in this verse includes the disorderly element. Paul is setting an example of how to treat the disorderly as a brother (v.15). The desire of Paul was for oneness in the assembly in order to strengthen its testimony.

Verse 17. "The salutation of Paul with mine own hand" In the light of a forged letter in ch.2.2 the apostle authenticates the epistle with his own hand to assure the believers that it was genuine. It is generally accepted that Paul dictated his letters to another who wrote the letter with Paul concluding the epistle. The exceptions to this are the epistles to the Galatians (*cf.* 6.11) and Philemon (*cf.* V.19).

"which is a token in every epistle" The word translated 'token' (*semeion*) means a sign or indication. There are two suggestions in regard to what is referred to here:- (1) The autograph of the apostle attached to the epistle. However Paul's signature is not attached to every one of his epistles. (2) The closing salutation which characterises Pauline epistles. The latter suggestion is more plausible. However it does not mean that every epistle would have the same closing salutation, but rather that each epistle would close with a salutation.

"So I write" What he was doing in closing this epistle was what he intended to do in future epistles. Only the first epistle to the Thessalonians predated this epistle so most of his epistles were not yet written. No other writer in the New Testament ends his epistles like Paul.

Verse 18. "The grace of our Lord Jesus Christ be with you all. Amen" The apostle concludes the epistle as he commenced, i.e. with grace (1.2). In so doing he uses the full title of the Lord as he does in concluding his first epistle. Paul desired that a sense of divine favour, which abundantly bestowed His blessing, be their enjoyed portion. Grace was the enabling power necessary for them to bear a harmonious and collective testimony for God in spite of the adverse circumstances they were in. This final statement is identical to the closing statement of his first epistle with the word 'all' added to it. As in v.16 Paul embraces all in the assembly including the disorderly. Every believer today needs the grace of God to faithfully live for Him, in keeping with His word, in this present godless environment.